The Creole French housewives were extremely frugal, no matter how wealthy their husbands might be. They occasionally sent the cook to the French Market for fresh vegetables, but more often they went themselves. They carried a large market basket, and checked everything very carefully for quality and price. They were sometimes accompanied by a servant, and probably made a trip almost every morning, to be sure their food was fresh. ♠ *All nationalities met at the market. When they spoke about the produce that was arriving in New Orleans from the surrounding country and also from ships coming into the port, they spoke in soft southern tones, and gently slurred over their words. Accents from the Irish Channel and from France, Italy, Spain and Africa were incorporated into words, and through the years, New Orleans has been so shortened, that it now sounds like "N'Awlins." If you say "Noo Orleens," the natives will barely understand you. We are not energetic in the south, so we tend to pronounce words with as few syllables as possible.*

Stuffed Peppers

Preheat oven to 350 degrees. Wash and split 3 large bell peppers in half. Parboil for 2 minutes and drain. Melt 1 stick of butter in a large skillet. Sauté an onion, a rib of celery, and 4 sprigs of parsley, all of which have been finely chopped. Add ½ pound of small fresh shrimp and ½ teaspoon thyme. Dampen half a loaf of stale French bread in a bowl, squeeze out excess water, and stir 3 eggs into it with 1 teaspoon garlic powder and salt and pepper. Stir sautéed ingredients into bread mixture and stuff pepper halves. Sprinkle with bread crumbs, dot with butter and place on baking sheet under medium flame in broiler for 20 minutes until lightly browned. Serves 6.

Recipe by Bobby Potts

The people who brought produce to the market would have been farming close to the Mississippi River or on the banks of some small bayou nearby, where the soil was rich and well watered. They would have had a stall in the market and their vegetables and fruit would be decoratively displayed. Any land far from the river would have tended to be too swampy. Meat, fish and game would have been brought to market, as well as herbs and flowers. The market had its beginning in 1791, and it hasn't changed all that dramatically in the meantime. The individual stalls, colorfully displaying their fresh merchandise, are still just as inviting to us.

Eggplant and Tomato Casserole

¼ cup salad oil
1 medium onion, chopped
¾ pound mushrooms, sliced
½ medium green pepper, chopped
1 medium eggplant, peeled and cut in 1" cubes
1 can (1 pound) plum tomatoes
1 tablespoon chopped parsley
1 teaspoon salt
2 eggs, beaten
1 cup each grated Parmesan and Mozzarella cheese

Use large fry pan, heat oil, and add onions, mushrooms and pepper. Sauté over medium heat until vegetables are soft (about 2 minutes). Stir in eggplant, tomatoes and parsley. Season with salt to taste. Cover and simmer slowly until eggplant is tender (25 minutes), stirring often. Uncover and increase heat, if needed, to reduce liquid. Stir Parmesan and Mozzarella cheese into beaten eggs. Spoon half of the eggplant mixture into 2½ quart casserole and top with half the cheese mixture. Repeat layers, ending with cheese. Bake uncovered in 375 degree oven for 30 minutes. If prepared ahead and cold, bake 45 minutes.

Stuffed Artichokes

5 large artichokes, seasoned
½ cup seasoned bread crumbs
5 cloves garlic, finely cut
8 ounces olive oil
1 finely chopped onion
½ cup parsley flakes
1 cup grated Romano cheese
  salt and pepper to taste

Snip off pointed ends of artichoke leaves, wash well, turn upside down, and drain thoroughly. Mix dry ingredients together in a bowl. Scoop bread crumb mixture into artichokes, separating leaves as you do. Place in a large pot of shallow salt water. Pour olive oil gently over the tops of the artichokes. Boil covered for about 1 hour.

Recipes by Bobby Potts

Red Cabbage

1 small head red cabbage
1 large red onion
3 Granny Smith apples
¼ cup butter or margarine
¼ cup balsamic vinegar
¼ cup brown sugar
¼ cup red wine
  salt and pepper to taste

Remove outer loose leaves of cabbage. Slice shred it very thinly. Core apples and cut onion apples in thin slices. Heat butter, and place onions to sauté lightly. Then add apples and cover with sliced red cabbage. Add all of the other ingredients cover the pot and simmer for about 1 hour. Remove the lid and add water as necessary. Taste to see the balance between sugar and vinegar suits y and correct accordingly. Serve hot as a side dish with other German dishes.

Bread had to be baked in the traditional manner of the French, long loaves of "Pain Ordi-
naire" or Common French Bread, often called "baguettes." The bakers would also have come
from France and could supply the real thing. And so it is today with La Madeleine, a bakery
that has recently come to New Orleans from France and is located on Jackson Square, close to
the French Market, as in the early days. The loaves are baked in a traditional brick oven.
Many shops are on the ground floor of the Pontalba apartments, which are located on both
sides of the square and were built in the 1850's.

New Orleans French Bread

nkle 2 packages Fleischmann's dry yeast over
er and stir until bubbly. (Do not use the rapid
g kind)

cups lukewarm water (85-105 degrees F.)
cups white flour (approximate measure)
easpoons salt
easpoons water
cornmeal
vegetable shortening
egg white
ablespoon water

othing about bread making is exact. Measuring is
important. You do not have to stretch, flatten,
roll this bread to make the shape. Just shape it
your hands and lay it in the pan.

a large bowl, sprinkle yeast over warm water
stir with a wooden spoon until yeast becomes
my, about 3 minutes. Add 4 cups of the flour
up at a time) mixing thoroughly between addi-
s. Beat mixture with spoon about 100 times,
ing the bowl ¼ turn after each 25 whips. Add
and water mixture and continue beating until
bined. Don't worry about lumps.

dd more flour, ¼ cup at a time, until dough starts
ing the sides of the bowl and forms a ball.
ove from bowl and knead on a floured surface,
ng more flour as needed. Place dough in a large
sed bowl, cover tightly with plastic wrap, and

place on a shelf in oven with oven light as the only
source of heat for 1¼ hours. (Don't over flour).

Turn back plastic wrap, return dough to floured
surface, punch down and knead for 2-3 minutes
(it will be a little sticky). Return to bowl, re-cover
and let rise again for 1 hour (it should feel very
fluffy and sound squeaky because of the air in it. It
will not be sticky at the end). When kneading,
always turn in the same direction. You are develop-
ing the gluten. Knead until the bread rejects the
flour. It should not be sticky. Don't over knead and
have too much flour in it.

continued on next page

Today, we associate Gumbo with both Creole and Cajun cultures, but Gumbo was created by the black slaves that were sent to New Orleans. They brought the vegetable Okra with them, which they called "Gombo," and made a sort of soup with it. The viscous juice in the seed pod acted as a thickener for the soup, which the Creoles then called Gumbo, because it was quite thick and different from soup. Later, they discovered the herb "filé" which was made from leaves of the sassafras tree, and it not only flavored the gumbo, but also acted as a thickening agent. They learned this from the Indians and, of course, they also made tea from the bark of the root of the sassafras tree. The Gumbo Shop is the place to go.

New Orleans French Bread *continued*

About ½ hour later or when dough has doubled in size, turn dough out of bowl. Punch down. Cut the dough into 2 pieces of equal size, forming each into a ball, and let rest for 5 minutes before shaping because cutting shocks the bread and disturbs the gluten. Shape the loaves and put into pans that have been prepared with shortening and sprinkled generously with cornmeal. It is good to use perforated pans to allow the bottom to brown. Cover loaves with a loosely woven cloth or loose plastic and let rise until loaves have doubled in size.

Preheat oven to 450 degrees F. Cut diagonal slits in top of loaves with a kitchen knife to let the air come out. Brush tops with egg white, beaten with a fork in a tablespoon of water. Bake for 30 min on middle shelf of oven. Don't paint it more t once and do not use the yolk.

Turn loaves upside-down, either in pans or dire onto oven shelf, and bake an additional 5 minu Remove to rack and cool.

Wait 20-30 minutes after taking the bread ou the oven to cut it. Let cool to room temperat wrap it in aluminum foil, and then you can free: if you wish.

Recipe by Chef

Creole Chicken Gumbo

1 large chicken, cut up
4 tablespoons cooking oil
1 large onion, chopped
2 quarts chicken stock, heated
2 tablespoons parsley, minced
2 tablespoons green onions, chopped
1 teaspoon chopped thyme, if fresh
　　½ teaspoon if dry
1 clove garlic, minced
3 bay leaves
1 pound smoked sausage (or andouille)
1 pint oysters
1 tablespoon filé powder
　cayenne pepper to taste
　salt and pepper to taste

Use a heavy pot, iron if possible, and brown chicken slowly in oil. Remove the chicken. Sa the onion until soft. Return chicken and any j that has drained off to the pot with onions. Co and cook on low heat for about 10 minutes, stirr occasionally to prevent burning. Add the hea stock, parsley, green onion, garlic, and bay leav Season generously with thyme. Add salt and pep to taste. Cook over low heat until chicken is ten Precook sausage for 10 minutes, add oysters a oyster water and cook for 10 minutes more. Rem from the fire and immediately add the filé pow stirring while adding. Serve immediately in la bowls, pouring it over steamed rice.

Some of the restaurants in New Orleans have been there for three or four generations. The Gumbo Shop is one of the older ones. They feature excellent Gumbos, but they also have a complete menu of Creole and Cajun dinners. One walks through a picturesque courtyard with a black iron fountain to enter the restaurant.

Oysters Roland

unch parsley
ound butter
easpoon black pepper
easpoon salt
loves garlic
welve ounce can mushrooms
  pieces and stems with juice
up bread crumbs
easpoon nutmeg
ozen parboiled oysters

lend in a high speed food processor such as Cuisi-
t in this order: parsley, garlic, and mushrooms.
nd well until parsley is finely chopped; then add
shroom juice and bread crumbs and finish blend-
; well. If this type of food processor is not
ilable, a meat grinder may be substituted using
  smallest plate for grinding parsley, garlic and
shrooms and blending afterward with a mixer.
lace 6 parboiled oysters (don't overcook) each in
" au gratin dish, smooth butter mixture over it,
 put under broiler until brown and bubbly. Makes
ut 10 servings.

Recipe by Christian's

Shrimp, Okra, and Tomato Gumbo

2 tablespoons cooking oil
1 pound fresh okra, topped and sliced in rounds
4 fresh tomatoes, chopped
1 onion, chopped finely
1 bell pepper, chopped
1 stalk celery, minced
1 clove garlic, minced
¼ cup chopped parsley
½ teaspoon basil
3 cups chicken broth
1 quart water
1 tablespoon Worcestershire Sauce
1 tablespoon vinegar
  salt and cayenne pepper to taste
2 pounds shrimp

Heat oil in a metal pot, add okra and smother, stirring so that it doesn't stick, until okra is dry and seeds turn pink. The gelatinous material will disappear. Add tomatoes. Continue to smother. Meanwhile, sauté onions, pepper, celery and garlic in separate pan until soft. When you have almost made a paste of the okra and tomatoes, add the sautéed vegetables and herbs and stir it well. Now add the chicken broth, water, Worcestershire Sauce and vinegar. Cook until it has thickened somewhat, about 30 minutes, and season to taste. Add deveined shrimp and cook about 10 minutes. If the shrimp cook too long, they will become rubbery. Add a Roux, if desired (see page 16).

Recipe by Bobby Potts

This is a typical French Quarter street scene, with all of the buildings touching each other. There was no room for a lawn or yard, as space on dry land was precious, but there was always a courtyard in the rear. The usual plan was to have the family business on the ground floor, and their living quarters upstairs. The rosy terra cotta colored building in the center is Brennan's restaurant. This was the first of the Brennan Family restaurants.

Poulet Rochambeau

2 two and one-half pound chickens
  seasoned flour
1½ sticks butter
1 cup minced green onions
1 teaspoon minced garlic
2 tablespoons flour
2 cups chicken stock
½ cup chopped mushrooms
1 tablespoon Worcestershire Sauce
½ teaspoon salt
  dash of cayenne pepper
½ cup Burgundy wine
4 Holland Rusks
¼ pound sliced, boiled ham
½ cup Bearnaise Sauce (see recipe at right)
  paprika

Disjoint and bone chicken, using neck, skin and bones to make stock. Dredge chicken in seasoned flour and sauté in butter until golden brown and tender. Keep warm in a covered dish. Sauté shallots and garlic in remaining butter. Add flour and brown well. Blend in stock, add mushrooms, and simmer 15 minutes. Add Worcestershire Sauce, salt, cayenne pepper and wine and mix thoroughly. Arrange Holland Rusks on a platter and cover with ham slices. Pour chicken sauce over ham. Arrange chicken pieces on the sauce and cover them with the Bearnaise Sauce. Dust the top with paprika. Serves 4.

Bearnaise Sauce

2 pounds butter
  lemon juice from 1½ lemons
½ teaspoon cayenne pepper
8 egg yolks
2 tablespoons red vinegar
1 teaspoon salt
½ teaspoon chopped parsley
⅛ teaspoon each chopped chives and tarragon lea▮

Melt butter in a small sauce pan and clarify. Pl▮ egg yolks in stainless steel bowl. Add lemon jui▮ vinegar, pepper and salt. Place bowl in a large sa▮ pan with boiling water, or over a double boiler. W▮ egg yolks until they thicken to form a soft pe▮ Remove from water. Slowly pour butter into e▮ Add it by degrees with a ladle until all is add▮ Quickly stir in herbs. Reserve in a warm place ▮ immediate usage. (This can be kept hot in a therm▮ until ready to use.)

Recipes by Brenn▮

Chicken Ratatouille

6 boneless chicken breasts (8-10 ounces each)
1 onion, diced
2 eggplants, diced
2 zucchini, diced
10 fresh mushrooms, sliced
2 green peppers, diced
4 cloves garlic, minced
½ cup olive oil
1 teaspoon each of thyme, oregano, marjoram,
   basil, and fennel
1 bay leaf
1 small can tomato paste
3 ripe tomatoes, diced
  salt and pepper to taste
(fennel has a strong anise flavor and is optional)

Sauté all vegetables in olive oil until tender, a▮ seasonings and tomato paste. Salt and pepper ▮ taste. Add 1 can of water with tomato paste ca▮ Cook slowly for 30 minutes. Season chicken brea▮ dust in flour and sauté in butter until brown and te▮ der. Serve over a bed of vegetables.

Recipe by Bobby P▮

DOWN BY THE FRENCH MARKET

Tujague's is one of the oldest restaurants in the Quarter, and is across the street from the French Market. It has kept a traditional menu and moderate prices, because it was always a family restaurant where Papa could take Mama and the children, or where he could take his business associates. As with many of the early French Restaurants, it has a partially pre-planned menu and one is offered a choice of entrees. Tujague's was always beloved by the Creoles and was famous for its beef brisket with horseradish sauce.

Bread Pudding
with Cranberry Brandy Sauce

1 loaf stale French Bread
1 quart milk
3 eggs
1 cup fresh apple, chopped
2 cups sugar
1 cup raisins
2 tablespoons vanilla
3 tablespoons margarine
1 can whole cranberries
    with juice
1 cup corn syrup
½ cup brandy

Soak stale bread in milk. Crush with hands until well mixed. Add eggs, sugar, vanilla and fruit. Pour margarine in bottom of thick pan and bake until very firm. Let cool and serve in squares or individual sherbet dishes. While pudding is baking, put cranberries with juice and corn syrup in a pan and heat. Cook down until mixture comes to a boil and cranberries become small and firm. Lower fire if boiling becomes too vigorous. Add brandy and continue to heat and stir until blended. Serve hot over pudding.

Recipe version by Bobby Potts

Tujague's serves one of the most elegant bread puddings I have ever eaten.

Brennan's Restaurant, shown in the picture on page six, started a family of restaurateurs; a. did Galatoire's, which was always famous for its Shrimp Remoulade and Trout Marguery, although other restaurants also serve these dishes. The children grew up in the restauran. atmosphere, so it was only natural for them to start restaurants of their own.

Crabmeat Yvonne

2 pounds fresh lump crabmeat
6 fresh artichoke bottoms, boiled and sliced
1 pound fresh mushrooms, sliced
½ cup clarified butter
  salt and pepper to taste

In a large skillet, sauté the mushrooms, then add the artichoke bottoms and crabmeat. Sauté gently until heated thoroughly. Season with salt and white pepper. Garnish with finely chopped parsley. Serve over toast points and with a lemon wedge. Serves 6.

Crêpes Maison

8 six-inch dessert crêpes
8 tablespoons currant jelly
6 tablespoons toasted, sliced almonds
  peel of 1 orange and 1 lemon, slivered
  powdered sugar
4 jiggers Grand Marnier

Roll 1 tablespoon currant jelly on each crêpe. Place 2 crêpes on each of 4 oven proof plates. Top with sliced almonds, orange and lemon peel, and sprinkle with powdered sugar. Pass under broiler until hot. Pour 1 jigger of Grand Marnier over each serving. Serves 4.

Godchaux Salad

In a large bowl combine:
  1 head iceberg lettuce, cubed
  2 large tomatoes, cubed
  1 pound backfin lump crabmeat
30-35 large shrimp, boiled and peeled

In a small bowl combine:
  5 ounces salad oil
  5 ounces red wine vinegar
  4 ounces Creole mustard

Mix dressing well, pour over salad and toss. Divide salad onto 4 chilled plates and garnish each with ½ sieved hard-boiled egg and 2 anchovies. Serves 4 as an entree, or more as a side salad.

Recipes by Leon Galatoire

Bananas Foster

4 tablespoons butter
½ teaspoon cinnamon
4 bananas, cut in ½ lengthwise, then halved
1 cup brown sugar
4 tablespoons banana liqueur
4 scoops vanilla ice cream
¼ cup Rum

Melt the butter over an alcohol burner (or ste can) in a flambé pan or attractive skillet. Add sugar, cinnamon and banana liqueur and stir to n Heat for a few minutes, then place the halv bananas in the sauce and sauté until soft. Add rum and allow it to heat well, then tip the pan so t the flame from the burner causes the sauce to ign Allow the sauce to flame until it dies out, tipping pan with a circular motion to prolong the flami. Serve over vanilla ice cream. First, lift the banar carefully out of the pan and place 4 pieces over ea portion of ice cream then spoon the hot sauce fr the pan over the bananas and ice cream. The trick this dish is to wait until the rum gets hot, so that y get a good flame when it is ignited. This can also prepared over a stove burner, then brought to table and flamed.

Recipe by Brenne

alatoire's is typical of the early restaurants of New Orleans. They were simple, with white
led floors and white table cloths. Galatoire's is lined with wall to wall mirrors that give a
ght, airy, spacious effect, and adds to the ambience although there are no other decorative
atures. If you don't arrive early for lunch, you are apt to find yourself waiting in line out-
de the door.

eafood Stuffed Eggplant Casserole

hole medium size eggplant
edium size shrimp, boiled
nces crabmeat
blespoons fresh parsley
allion (shallot or green onion)
read crumbs and Parmesan cheese

n Sauce:
blespoons butter
vel tablespoons flour
blespoons milk

lve the eggplant, bake in pan with water for 30
tes or until tender. Make the cream sauce by
ling the flour into the melted butter and gradual-
ding milk. Let cool. Remove the pulp from the
of the cooked eggplant (gently so as not to tear
hell). Sauté the chopped pulp, scallion, parsley,
p and crabmeat together. Add the cream sauce
cook all together until heated through. Spoon
ng into reserved shells of eggplant. Sprinkle
bread crumbs and Parmesan cheese and bake till
are brown. Serves 2-4, depending on how much
ove this dish.

Shrimp Remoulade

1 pound shrimp, boiled, peeled and deveined
⅔ cup olive oil
5 tablespoons Creole mustard
1 bunch green onions
2 tablespoons paprika
⅓ cup vinegar
1 stalk celery
2 cloves garlic
1 bunch parsley
  dash of Tabasco
1 tablespoon prepared horseradish

In a food processor fitted with a steel blade, chop all
vegetables very fine. Remove to a ceramic or glass
bowl and add mustard, paprika, horseradish, Tabasco
and salt and black pepper to taste. Add vinegar and
gradually add olive oil while whisking. Fold in
shrimp and let marinate several hours or overnight in
refrigerator. Serve cold over shredded lettuce.

Trout Marquery

1 two and one-half pound trout
1 tablespoon olive oil
1 cup water
2 sticks butter
3 egg yolks
  juice of 1 lemon, strained
  salt, pepper and cayenne
12 shrimp
2 truffles
½ can mushrooms

Skin and filet trout and place the folded filets
in a pan with olive oil and water. Bake in a
hot oven about 15 minutes. See recipe for
Hollandaise Sauce on page 12. Add the seasoning, shrimp, truffles and mushrooms (cut
into small pieces) to sauce and pour over fish.
It is nice to flute creamed potatoes around the
edge of the plate and run it under the broiler to
barely brown the top. Then place the fish and
sauce in the center and serve. (Note: This is
not called Trout "Margery").

Recipes by Leon Galatoire

New Orleans is a place of many churches, for the spiritual life of the city is very much alive. There are cathedrals and many small churches of all denominations. St. Louis Cathedral is undoubtedly the most famous, and it is worth the crick you will get in your neck to go in and view the paintings on the ceiling. On the plaza in front of the church, continuous entertainment is going on, and the hot dog wagon is usually parked on the corner. There is no lack of food because there are restaurants and ice cream parlors on both sides of Jackson Square, which the church faces. There are also mimes and musicians, dancers and painters, and any other artist who care to put on a show there for a small donation dropped in a hat or a violin case.

Duck Blackberry Vinegar

2 ducks four-five pounds average
4-6 ounces blackberry vinegar
12 ounces demi-glace
4-6 ounces butter

To prepare blackberry vinegar, use one part black-berries to two parts white vinegar. Soak the berries in the vinegar and pass the mixture through a food mill. Discard the seeds. Season the ducks inside and out. Roast them in a 350 degree oven for about 4 hours. When the ducks are almost done, turn up the oven to 500 degrees for 20 minutes. Remove the ducks from the oven and let them cool. When they are cool enough to touch, cut them in half and remove all the bones from each half. If you prefer, you can leave the 2 extremity bones in both the wing and the leg. Then place the ducks skin side up and heat them under a broiler until the skin is very crispy. Then place them in a 300 degree oven to keep warm. Combine the demi-glace (see recipe above) and the blackberry vinegar. Bring this to a boil and finish with butter. Spoon the sauce on the plate (preferably on individual plates) and place the duck on top of the sauce. Garnish with watercress and cracked black pepper sprinkled on top.

Demi-Glace

4 medium carrots, diced
1 large onion, coarsely chopped
  white portion of 2 medium leeks, coarsely chopped
2 cloves
  pinch of thyme, rosemary and a bay leaf
5 pounds veal and/or beef bones
1 small can tomato purée
2 quarts chicken stock

Roast bones in medium oven until browned. large stock pot, soften vegetables in butter until gl. or lightly browned. Add herbs and bones with w to cover and simmer with lid for 8 hours, checking uid level periodically. Strain stock and refrigerate.

Remove cooked meat and fat from bones and again for 8 hours. Strain, add tomato purée, chic stock and combine with previous stock. Sim without lid to reduce by ⅔ or more until li becomes a thick and rich beef glaze. It is impor to skim anything that comes to the top during reduction. Use as a base for the sauce.

Remoulade Sauce

6 bunches green onions
3 medium white onions
6 bunches parsley
6 bunches celery
1 quart red wine vinegar
1 gallon Creole mustard
3 ounces Tabasco
13 ounces Lea & Perrins
½ cup cayenne (red) pepper
½ cup salt
⅓ cup white pepper
1 gallon Wesson oil
2 cups paprika

Chop all vegetables in food processor. Mix other ingredients and all the vegetables. Check the strength of the cayenne. Additional caye may be necessary, depending on the strength of particular brand used. Large amount to keep awh

Recipes by Christ.

ristian's is a restaurant that has been established in an old church. Chris Ansel is a mem-
r of the Galatoire family mentioned previously, and Christian is really his name, but most
propriate for a restaurant that was established in a church. The food is delicious and
cludes some of the exotic examples of French cuisine which take so long to prepare well,
ch as Bouillabaisse and Terrine de Campagne.

Beurre Noir

ce 1 pound butter in a heavy aluminum pot and
; butter to a boil. Stir butter with a whisk
ently until dark brown. Remove from fire and
nue to cool by whisking.

*or's note: Some also fry the fish in butter, and con-
to brown the butter after the fish is done, if the but-
not dark enough, and then they pour that beurre noir
he fish. Either way is fine.)*

Recipes by Christian's

Trout Meuniere Amandine

Immerse filet of trout (6 ounces) in milk. Dust
with flour and deep fry until done. Top with Beurre
Noir and garnish with roasted sliced almonds. Heat
on dinner plate (most are oven proof for this proce-
dure) under broiler until lightly browned. Garnish
with chopped parsley and parsley sprig. (See page 22
for Bouillabaisse recipe from Christian's)

CREOLE COOKING FROM AN IRISH DYNASTY

*Breakfast at Brennan's has become a New Orleans tradition, although Brennan's is not as o[...]
as some of the French Restaurants in the city. There is a story, which is probably apocrypha[...]
that Brennan bet some of the French restaurateurs that he could run a French restaurant a[...]
well as they could. He has apparently proved his point, if this story is true, for other mem[...]
bers of the family have proved that they also can cook, not only in the Creole style, bu[...]
"Country Cajun" too. Mr. B's and Commander's Palace spring from the same family.*

Eggs Benedict

6 slices toast or Holland Rusk
6 slices boiled ham
6 eggs
   paprika
¾ cup Hollandaise Sauce

Place ham on toast and top with poached egg. Cover with Hollandaise Sauce and sprinkle with a dash of paprika. Serves 6.

With breakfast or a brunch, it is nice to serve a Mimosa, Bloody Mary, or a wonderful pale pink Ojen Cocktail.

Eggs Sardou

To make creamed spinach:
  1 cup butter
1½ cups chopped white onion
1¼ cups flour
  4 cups milk
  ½ teaspoon salt
  ½ teaspoon black pepper
  8 cups cooked spinach
16 large cooked artichoke bottoms, heated
16 poached eggs
     Hollandaise Sauce

To prepare the creamed spinach, melt butter [...] low heat in a heavy saucepan. Add the cho[...] onion and cook until just soft. Add the flour gr[...] ally, stirring constantly. Stir in the milk, [...] stirring, and cook until evenly blended and wa[...] through. Add the salt, pepper and spinach and [...] a few minutes more, just until the spinach is wa[...] through and the mixture evenly blended. Put [...] amounts of creamed spinach on eight heated p[...] then place artichoke bottoms on top of the spi[...] Place 2 poached eggs side by side on each artic[...] bottom, then ladle an even coating of Holland[...] over each portion.

Hollandaise Sauce

2 pounds butter
   lemon juice from 1½ lemons
½ teaspoon cayenne pepper
8 egg yolks
2 tablespoons red wine vinegar
1 teaspoon salt

Melt butter in a small sauce pan and clarify. [...] egg yolks in stainless steel bowl. Add lemon [...] vinegar, pepper and salt. Place bowl in a large [...] pan with boiling water, or over a double boiler. [...] egg yolks until they thicken to form a soft [...] Remove from water. Slowly pour butter into [...] Add it by degrees with a ladle, until all is a[...] Reserve in a warm place for immediate usage. [...] can be kept hot in a thermos until ready to use).

Recipes by Bren[...]

nother Brennan Family restaurant, Mr. B's, started out as a bistro. It has now become a full edged and well-qualified French restaurant. The food is as elegant and delicious as it ounds on the menu, which is always a pleasant surprise, and the service is faultless. Some f the presentations have a modern flare based on traditional French cooking. The atmoshere coordinates with that of the street scene, with the café curtains on the outside windows the diner can savor the passing parade as well as the food.

Angel Cake

gg whites
easpoons cream of tartar
easpoons salt
ablespoon vanilla
ups flour, sifted 5 times
ups sugar, sifted 3 times

tter and flour 3 nine-inch cake pans, with parch- paper on bottom. Sift ⅔ cup of the sugar in with lour. Make meringue: In a large mixer, beat egg es and salt until slightly frothy. Add cream of tar-Beat until soft peaks appear and gradually add the r. Beat until whites make stiff peaks. ld in flour, ¼ cup at a time. Do not stir. Bake at degrees with fan on until browned (or use a ection oven) about 8-10 minutes. Bake another 5 minutes until done. Garnish with fresh berries.

Mozzarella Garlic Bread

"Po'Boy" loaf of French Bread
ound butter
ablespoon chopped garlic
ablespoons chopped parsley
ups grated Mozzarella cheese

ften butter to almost the melting point. Add garlic parsley. Slice Po'Boy loaf in half lengthwise. h each half with garlic butter, then sprinkle with ed Mozzarella. Cut into 4" pieces and place in 450 ee oven on a baking sheet for about 8 minutes cheese is melted and outside of the bread is crisp.

Lemon Creme Sauce
for Angel Cake

10 egg yolks
1 cup sugar
1 quart cream
6-7 lemons (juice only)

(Author's note: This is actually a lemon "anglaise" sauce that is thin, creamy and pourable.)

Mix yolks and sugar together. Slowly add heated cream. Cook over water to thin anglaise consistency or until surface bubbles are gone. Cool to room temperature. Squeeze lemons into anglaise. Taste and adjust lemon. Strain. Keep at room temperature.

Pour over cake or pour into plate and gently lift cake onto the sauce. Place the fresh berries at the side or around the cake.

Petite Filet Mignon with Raisins

5½ ounce filet mignon
3 ounces veal stock
1 ounce brandy
2 tablespoons raisins
1 tablespoon sweet butter
coarse ground black pepper
salt to taste

The amounts of ingredients given above are for each filet.

Roll filet mignon in coarse pepper to coat, but not too heavily. Sauté filet in butter until rare. Remove from skillet to warm platter. Throw away excess grease in pan, deglaze the pan with brandy and add veal stock and raisins. Bring sauce to a boil, taste for seasoning, and add 1 tablespoon of butter to finish. Pour immediately over filet. Serve with wilted fresh spinach.

Wilted Spinach: In a large sauté pan, brown 1 tablespoon butter. Add 2 cups spinach, salt and pepper; toss quickly and remove from heat. Add a few drops of lemon juice. Spinach should be just wilted and not cooked through.

Recipes by Mr. B's

The Garden District was originally the habitat of the Americans that came to New Orleans. They were referred to as "Les Americains" by the Creoles, and they moved to the first settlement on the Mississippi that was above the Quarter. Later, some Creoles joined them in the new "subdivision." Another member of the Brennan family bought the old Commander Palace in that area and made a magnificent success of it. They maintain a separate chef for each of the specialized cuisines of Louisiana. Thus, another Irish family made a mark in the business of French style food.

Hickory Grilled Duckling

½ boned duckling (weight before cooking - 4 pounds)

Ducks are roasted slowly, well seasoned with Creole meat seasoning on skin, fresh cloves of garlic and fresh rosemary in cavity. Ducks are completely boned and, on order, are grilled on a hot hickory grill that permeates the meat with a mild smoke flavor and renders off excess fat from the duckling.

The sauce is simply a fond du canard, achieved by reducing a duck sauce until it has strength and character, adding sprigs of fresh rosemary for fragrance. *(Author's note: This is something like a demi-glace cooked down from duck stock, made with bones, etc. See recipe.)*

When the duck comes off the grill, it is placed in a sauté pan and finished in a 450 degree oven for approximately 8 minutes. The duck is held on a warm serving platter. The sauté pan is deglazed with brandy, the fond du canard is added, and the sauce is further reduced and finished with butter.

The duckling is served crisp, yet the meat is still slightly pink. The aroma of the hickory and the natural sauce with rosemary makes the dish unique, yet simple and flavorful.

Romaine, Roquefort and Bacon Sa

2 small heads of Romaine, torn into 2" pieces
   rinsed and drained
8 strips of bacon, cooked and coarsely chopped
5 ounces Roquefort cheese, crumbled
¾ cup vinaigrette and 1 egg yolk

In a stainless steel bowl, add egg yolk and w bacon with 1 tablespoon grease and Roque cheese. Whisk in the vinaigrette dressing, addi slowly, emulsifying the dressing. Toss in Romaine leaves, coating them well with the dress Distribute onto 4 plates, being sure to have bi Roquefort and bacon divided among each salad.

Pasta Jambalaya

3 ounces melted butter (to sauté)
1 pound andouille sausage
6 ounces cooked duck breast
6 ounces raw chicken - sliced thin
18 or more large shrimp
⅔ cup diced onions
⅔ cup diced pepper (red and green)
⅔ cup ripe tomatoes
2½ cups veal stock
1 pound cold sweet butter pieces
   spinach pasta (cooked)
3 teaspoons chopped garlic
1 teaspoon red pepper flakes
3 teaspoons Creole Seasoning

Add andouille, duck meat, chicken, shrimp, on garlic and pepper to hot sauté pan with melted bu Sauté over high flame, stirring with fork and sha pan. When shrimp are half cooked through (abc minutes), add veal stock, tomatoes and seasor Reduce by ⅓.

Swirl in cold butter pieces, continuously stir with a fork and rotating sauté pan until all butt incorporated (sauce should be smooth and lig Place warm pasta in bowl, pour jambalaya mix over it, and serve immediately. *(Author's note: In the restaurant, this is made upon o 1 serving at a time. I have expanded it to serve 6.)*

Recipes by M.

from the early days of fine restaurants in the Vieux Carré, which translates "Old Quarter," the Creoles have loved their flaming desserts. Crêpe Suzettes, Cherries Jubilee, and Bananas Foster all qualify for such spectacular productions, but Café Diable was the perfect finish for any grand meal of rich Creole foods. It just seemed to settle everything into place. An oft quoted recipe comes to us from Talleyrand who said coffee must be "Pur comme un ange, ouce comme l'amour, noir comme le diable, chaud comme l'enfer." (Pure as an angel, sweet s love, black as the devil, and hot as hell).

Café Brulot or Café Diable

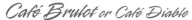

ups really strong coffee (with or without chicory)
mon
eedless orange
oves
ick cinnamon
mps sugar
up Cognac
up Grand Marnier, Curacao, or Triple Sec for the
 orange flavor

lemon in half. Cut orange in half and spike with
s and cinnamon stick. Place these halves in chafing
(or pan on the stove), pour liqueurs over them, and
gently. Add a little grated or thinly sliced peel and
clarify in the warming liquid. Put 8 cubes of sugar
 pan and ladle. Pour a little Cognac in the ladle,
by holding a match under it, and then ignite. Pour
urning liqueur from ladle into pan and let it all flame
before slowly adding hot coffee. Serve after flame
down. Always remember that if you add very much
alcoholic liquid too soon or too fast to the alcoholic
nt of a recipe that is to be ignited, the flaming spec-
will not last long enough to truly enhance the taste.

Crêpes Suzettes

4 rounded tablespoons flour
½ teaspoon sugar
2 eggs
1 cup milk
2 tablespoons cooled melted butter
 pinch of salt

Put flour, 1 egg and egg yolk, salt, sugar and 4 tablespoons milk into a bowl. Beat with a whisk until quite smooth. Then add remainder of milk and cooled, melted butter. Mix in beaten egg white, cover and let stand in refrigerator at least ½ hour. Any type of crêpe pan may be used, and after crêpes are browned lightly, they should be stacked on a cake rack. Spread each thin pancake on one side with some orange butter, made as follows: Cream butter with a little sugar and the grated rind of 1 orange and mix in a little Grand Marnier and Cognac. Fold the crêpes once in half and once again into quarter sections or roll up and set aside.

Sauce: 3 naval oranges
                ¾ cup granulated sugar
                ½ cup butter or margarine
                6 sugar cubes
                ¼ cup Grand Marnier
                ⅛ cup Cognac

Put the following in a chafing dish: butter, sugar, sugar cubes (which have been rubbed on the outside of an orange), orange juice, and finely grated rind of another orange, the Grand Marnier and the Cognac. Simmer gently until rind is translucent, then add skinned sections of one orange and put crêpes in to gently heat through. Add more Grand Marnier and Cognac if necessary. Warm a little Cognac in a ladle by holding a match under it and then light it. Pour lighted Cognac in and flame ingredients in chafing dish thoroughly. Do not use too much juice or mixture will not flame. Fresh or canned mandarin or tangerine sections may be used instead of orange sections.

Recipes by Bobby Potts

The dining room of any restaurant is where the end product is produced and the skill of the people in the kitchen determines the quality of the presentation on the plate. New Orleans sure has as fine a collection of chefs as almost any city in the United States. The chefs at Arnaud produced a tremendous assortment of some of the finest food in New Orleans for our picture.

Veal Wohl

18 slices of top quality baby veal
     (approximately 1 ounce each)
 1 cup flour
 1 cup butter
 3 cups sautéed lump crabmeat
 3 cups Crawfish O'Connor
1½ cups Port Wine Sauce
 1 tablespoon chopped parsley
 6 cherry tomatoes
    salt and pepper to taste

Veal Stock

 1 pound veal bones
 ½ tablespoon rock salt
 ¾ gallon water
 1 white onion, unpeeled, halved
 1 cup carrots, chopped coarsely
 1 cup leeks, chopped coarsely
 1 cup celery, chopped coarsely
 ½ cup chopped parsley
    pinch of thyme
 1 bay leaf
 1 tablespoon black pepper
 1 clove garlic, chopped
1½ cups tomato purée
 2 tablespoons roux

Place the veal bones in a toasting pan, sprinkle with rock salt. Bake at 350 degrees until brown. In a large skillet, blacken the onion face down to caramelize the natural sugars. Combine all the ingredients in a large stock pot. Bring to a boil. Reduce to 1 quart in volume. Thicken with roux to coat spoon. Strain.

Roux

½ pound butter
½ pound flour

Melt butter in a small pot over high heat. Add flour gradually, stirring constantly with wire whip. Cook until mixture becomes a paste. Remove from heat. Store covered at room temperature until needed. Do not refrigerate.

(All of the recipes on these 2 pages are used in Veal Wohl)
Recipes by Arnaud's

Americaine Sauce

 4 pounds crawfish with shell on
 ½ cup olive oil
 ¾ cup shallots, chopped
 ¼ cup white onions, chopped
 ¼ cup carrots, sliced
 ¼ cup celery, chopped
 ¼ cup leeks, chopped
 ¼ cup Brandy
 6 tablespoons white wine
 2 tablespoons tomato purée
 2 ounce tomato, whole
 1 ounce garlic, whole
 4 cloves
 ½ teaspoon black peppercorns
 2 cups fish or chicken stock (see page 18)
 2 teaspoons lobster base
 2 quarts water
 2 ounces roux
    salt, pepper and cayenne pepper to taste
(See recipe for Roux)

Wash shellfish several times. Heat olive oil over heat to smoking point. Add crawfish. Cook until Add vegetables and stir 3-4 minutes. Add brandy flame 10 seconds. Extinguish by placing cover pot. Add wine, tomato purée, tomato, garlic, c and peppercorns. Stir. Add fish stock, lobster base water. Bring to a boil. Reduce heat, cover and si for 30 minutes. Blend in blender for 2 minutes. R to pot and boil 7-10 minutes. Thicken with roux sauce coats spoon. Strain. Season to taste.

Port Wine Sauce

½ cup shallots, chopped
   Bouquet garni (see page 57)
 2 cups Port wine
 ½ gallon veal stock
 2 tablespoons roux

Heat a pot over high heat. Add shallots, Bouquet and wine. Reduce to ½ volume. Add veal stock above left) and bring to a boil. Reduce heat and si for 10 minutes. Thicken with roux until sauce coat spoon. Strain and season to taste. Yields 1 quart.

Arnaud's Restaurant has a long history in the French Quarter. Count Arnaud's residence was located on Esplanade, which was the lower limit of the Quarter. The Esplanade was where the elegant people had town houses and strolled in the evening when the summer air was cooled somewhat by the breezes from the river. The Casbarians bought Arnaud's after Count Arnaud's daughter died, and restored it to its former elegance. Again, the traditions of marvelous French food are preserved and handed down.

Crawfish O'Connor

3 pounds boiled crawfish tails
2 tablespoons butter
1⅛ cups chopped shallots
6 tablespoons Brandy
6 tablespoons whipping cream
   salt, pepper and cayenne to taste
   pinch of parsley

Melt butter in a sauté pan over high heat. Add shallots and cook until transparent. Add crawfish. Flame with Brandy. Add whipping cream and bring to a boil. Reduce heat and simmer for 3 minutes. Add salt, pepper and cayenne pepper to taste. Sprinkle chopped parsley on top before serving.

Ralph and Kacoo's started as a small restaurant on the island side of an oxbow lake calle False River. It later moved to the side of the lake where the town of New Roads lies. The soon opened a restaurant in Baton Rouge, and eventually in New Orleans. These restaurant were huge successes. They now have been sold to a new owner. Cajun cooking was not foun much in New Orleans before World War II. Most of the restaurant menus prior to that liste the more traditional Creole dishes. However, after some of the Cajuns got "out of the woods and saw the world, they began to migrate to New Orleans and open restaurants. The cit slickers got a taste of good hot seasonings, and it was a whole new love affair with food.

Crawfish Salad

2 cups crawfish, cooked and peeled
4-5 cups lettuce, chopped
2 tablespoons Thousand
   Island dressing
1 tablespoon mayonnaise
¼ cup green onions, chopped
¼ cup green peppers, chopped fine
½ cup celery, chopped
1 teaspoon sweet pickle relish
1 tablespoon creamy garlic dressing
1 teaspoon salt (or to taste)
   dash of red pepper

Use well-chilled ingredients. Combine all together and toss. Serve on a large curly lettuce leaf.

Recipe by Kacoo Olinde

Crawfish au Gratin

1 cup chopped onions
1 cup chopped celery
½ cup chopped green bell pepper
½ cup chopped red bell pepper
½ pound butter or margarine
¼ cup flour
2 pounds crawfish tails
4 cups cream, warmed
1 cup grated cheddar cheese
½ cup burgundy
   salt and black or cayenne pepper to taste

Fish Stock

2 pounds fish bones
1 cup shallots, coarsely chopped
2 cups leeks, coarsely chopped
1 cup parsley, chopped
1 cup celery, coarsely chopped
   pinch of thyme
1 bay leaf
1 teaspoon black pepper
2½ cups white wine
1 gallon water

Onions, celery, and bell peppers are so often used in Cajun dishes that the chefs refer to them as the "Holy Trinity." The hot taste of pepper and pepper sauce is referred to as the devil. Melt butter over lowered heat. Sauté all vegetables until softened. Slowly blend in flour and warmed cream. Add wine as sauce thickens and simmer until the consistency is creamy. Add seasonings and a pinch of thyme if desired. You may place the crawfish tails in a large casserole or in individual baking dishes. Carefully pour cream sauce over crawfish and let it run down in. Sprinkle cheddar over top. Bake at 350 degrees until crusty and bubbly.

Wash fish bones several times to be sure they thoroughly clean. Place fish bones, vegetables and sonings in a large stock pot. Add wine and water. Reduce heat and simmer for 15 minutes. Remove heat, skim, and allow to cool. Strain. Yields 1 quar

Recipe by Arno

Ralph and Kacoo's restaurant in New Orleans was elaborately decorated to create a colorful atmosphere with country antiques, pictures of wildlife, and a feeling for the Gulf waters and the Bayou Country. Crawfish really became famous. With the spicy seasonings and colorful red bodies, they were the base of many appetizing dishes, and were even used as sauces and stuffings with meat dishes. As time went on, the old Creole restaurants began to add these dishes to their menus, and a marriage between Cajun and Creole was created.

Crawfish Etouffée

2 pounds crawfish tails
1 cup oil
¾ cup flour
1½ cups onions, chopped
¼ cup celery, chopped
⅓ cup garlic, mashed and minced
⅔ cup green peppers, chopped
¼ cup butter
½ cup tomato paste
1 can chicken broth
3 cups water
2 chicken flavored bouillon cubes
2 teaspoons salt
2 teaspoons black pepper
1 teaspoon Tabasco pepper sauce
1 teaspoon fancy paprika

In a large skillet, make roux by stirring oil and flour over slow to medium heat. When roux reaches peanut butter color, add chopped onions, celery, garlic and green peppers and sauté for 5 minutes. In another skillet (small) melt butter and add tomato paste. Sauté paste in butter until smooth and thick, about 5 minutes, and then mix with roux. Pour in broth, slowly add the water with the melted bouillon cubes in it, and balance of seasonings. Cook for 30 minutes. Add crawfish tails 5 minutes before serving. Serve with rice.

Recipes by Ralph and Kacoo's Restaurant

Baked Stuffed Flounder

up chopped celery
up chopped green onions with tops
love garlic, minced
ablespoons butter
up bread crumbs
ablespoons lemon juice
ound boiled shrimp, chopped
ound lump crabmeat
ablespoons chopped parsley
gg, slightly beaten
lack pepper or cayenne or both
alt to taste
lounders, medium size

auté celery, onion and garlic in melted butter over
heat. Add bread, crab, shrimp, parsley and egg
mix well. Season with salt and pepper. Split the
k side of the flounder, lengthwise and crosswise,
sen meat from bone of fish to form a pocket for
fing. Brush well with melted butter and lemon
e. Salt and pepper and stuff the pocket. Place in
with enough water to cover bottom of pan. Broil
from heat until fish flakes easily with a fork.
ste frequently with liquid in pan.

Olde N'Awlins Cookery was one of the first really successful and totally Cajun restaurants that opened in the Quarter. As the tourists walked into the Quarter from their hotels and hunted for new tastes on the side streets, they found this restaurant and went back and told their friends about it. It was a totally new experience. They even served Redfish Beignets (Fried fritter type inventions with pieces of succulent Redfish in them.) The menu was hand written on two blackboards, one inside near the big bar, and one in the pleasant courtyard hung near the palm trees. "Cajun" had really come to town to stay.

Lemon Crêpes

Crêpe Batter:
2 tablespoons flour
1 egg
1 cup milk
pinch of salt, nutmeg and cinnamon

Crêpe Filling:
8 ounces cream cheese (leave out at room temperature ahead of time)
4 tablespoons sugar
dash of rum
¾ teaspoon lemon zest (yellow outer part)

Mix together until well blended.

Lemon Sauce:
2 tablespoons lemon juice
6 tablespoons water
1 tablespoon sugar
1 tablespoon butter
1 tablespoon cornstarch dissolved in 2 tablespoons water

Putting Lemon Crêpes together:

Coat an 8" crêpe pan lightly with oil. Heat pan until a drop of water sizzles when dropped upon it. Then pour 2 tablespoons of crêpe batter in the pan, tilting it so that the batter covers entire bottom of pan. Cook the crêpes on one side only until golden brown.

Stack crêpes, brown side up, and cover with a damp cloth.

Put a large spoonful of cheese filling in the center of each crêpe, roll, and spoon Lemon Sauce over the top. Serve warm. Serves 6-8.

Recipe by Olde N'Awlins Cookery

Red Beans and Rice

2 cups (1 pound) dried red beans
1 good ham bone and small chunks of ham
1 onion, chopped
2½ quarts water
1 pod garlic
salt and Tabasco to taste

The red beans used in Louisiana are not the sa as kidney beans, but if you can't get anything e the kidney beans will work. Nothing gives red be the flavor that a good ham bone does. If you can pickled meat, use that in red beans and in gree Soak beans overnight in a quart of water in a he pot. Add another quart of water in the morning, ham and bone, the onion and the garlic. Add a li salt. Simmer slowly 3-4 hours, until the beans begin to break up and help thicken the red sauce, while most of them are still holding their shape. more salt and pepper to taste, and serve over fluffy rice. Leftover red beans can be made into s by putting them through a blender with some chicl bouillon and a little lemon juice. Stir in 1 tablespc of sherry per serving and sprinkle some chopp hard-boiled egg over the top with a sprig of parsley

n addition to the special dishes, there was even special bread. The old style baguettes of French Bread had been turned into alligators and other critters of the swamp. Alligator sausage had also come to town. New Orleans Creoles turned up their noses at such a thought, and tourists were timid about trying it. However, since the government began to allow harvesting of alligators and it was all perfectly legal, adventurous folks began to try it and found out that it was delicious. There was Alligator Gumbo, Alligator Sausage, Fried Alligator Appetizers, and Alligator Sauce Piquante over fluffy white rice.

Trout with Pecans
(Sometimes called Trout Pecaniere)

6 six ounce deboned trout filets
3 tablespoons Creole seasoning
2 cups flour
3 eggs (whole)
2 cups milk
1 teaspoon cayenne pepper
8 ounces clarified butter or oil
8 ounces roasted pecans
  pecan butter (below)
  Creole Meuniere sauce (below)

Season filets with 2 tablespoons of Creole seasoning. Make a wash of beaten eggs and milk. Season flour with 1 tablespoon of Creole seasoning and cayenne (red) pepper. Dredge filets in seasoned flour, then in egg-milk wash, then again in seasoned flour (double battered). Cover bottom of heavy skillet with ½" clarified butter and heat to 375 degrees. Sauté filets evenly on both sides until golden brown, turning once. It should take between 3½-4 minutes. Remove from skillet and drain. Evenly spread 1 tablespoon of pecan butter over filets. Sprinkle roasted pecans over the top. Pour 2 ounces of Meuniere sauce over pecans. Serve immediately. (Author's note: You may chop the pecans if you prefer). Serves 6.

Creole Meuniere Sauce

½ cup water or seafood stock
½ cup Worcestershire Sauce
  juice of 1 lemon
2 tablespoons flour mixed with water

Bring water (or stock), Worcestershire Sauce and lemon to a boil, whisk in light wash and return to boil. Whisk in softened butter (which helps thicken mixture). Hold in double boiler over low heat.

Recipes by Olde N'Awlins Cookery

Easiest and Best Way to Cook Rice

ring at least 3 quarts of well-salted water to a rapid Add 1 tablespoon of oil and 1 of vinegar to the r. Slowly add 1 cup of long grain rice which has picked over but not washed. Reduce heat and simfor exactly 18 minutes. The oil will keep the water boiling over, and the vinegar will let each grain "fall self" when served. Drain through a colander and off excess starch with cold water. Return to colanand steam over a little hot water in the pot for a few tes until well warmed again.

Recipe by Bobby Potts

Pecan Butter

blespoons roasted pecans
blespoons salted butter
aspoon Worchestershire Sauce
of 1 lemon

urée all ingredients in cuisinart to make the sauce as oth as possible.

Although the Quarter is known as the French Quarter, it is actually called the Vieux Carré in French, which means The Old Square, and the architecture is more Spanish than French. Much of the Quarter had burned at one time, and the reconstruction occurred during Spanish occupation. The lace balconies of intricately twined cast iron are the result of that influence. Some of the restaurants are fortunate enough to have the lacy iron balconies. One of these is Mike Anderson's, another restaurant that started out of town in Baton Rouge and expanded to a second restaurant in New Orleans. It offers some of the choicest seafood dishes available.

Bouillabaisse

This is one of the most fantastic and traditional of all New Orleans dishes, and its history goes back to Marseilles, France. Some attributed it to Venus, who they said, created it for her handsome husband Vulcan. But the French poet Mery wrote a long poem about Bouillabaisse, which begins as follows:

"Pour le vendredi maigre, un jour, certaine abbesse D'un couvent marseillais crea la bouill-abaisse." Translation: For a Friday abstinence meal, one day, a certain abbess of a Marseilles nunnery created the bouillabaisse.

He goes on to exclaim about the variety of fish used in it, where each kind feeds to make its own flavor, and how wonderful the overlay of all the flavors is. Many restaurants require that you order it in advance and some serve it only at certain times of the year because if several kinds of fish are used in it, the preparation becomes complicated. This recipe will be an easy one for you to prepare.

Heat ⅓ cup olive oil in a very large skillet and add 1 finely sliced onion. Sauté onion slices for a few minutes on medium fire until transparent.

Then add:
- 3 cloves garlic, chopped
- ½ bay leaf
- ¼ teaspoon thyme
- ⅛ teaspoon powdered anise
- 1 tomato, peeled with seeds removed and crushed
- ½ cup white wine
- 1½ quarts fish stock or chicken broth

Simmer uncovered until onions are tender (about 15-20 minutes).

Then add:
- 16 shrimp, peeled
- 12 oysters
- ¼ pound crabmeat or gumbo crabs
- 8 fish filets (trout, redfish, etc.)

and continue to simmer until the fish filets are tender. Do not overcook the fish filets. Add ¼ teaspoon powdered saffron. Serve the bouillabaisse immediately, very hot, in large soup plates with toasted garlic bread rounds and rouille (see below) in separate plates. Add some rouille to enhance the flavor of the bouillabaisse.

Garlic Bread Rounds: Cut French Bread into rounds (about 6 pieces per person), baste with olive oil and finely chopped garlic. Toast on tray under broiler until light brown.

Rouille: Make a regular mayonnaise, using 3 yolks (room temperature) and ½ quart olive oil, add one heaping teaspoon chopped garlic and ¾ spoon cayenne pepper.

Recipe by Christi

Strawberries Arnaud

- 3 cups sliced strawberries
- 3 cups vanilla ice cream
- 1½ cups Wine Sauce (see recipe next page)
- whipped cream

Place 1 scoop of ice cream in each of 6 champagne glasses. Cover with strawberries. Top with sauce and decorate with whipped cream.

Recipe by Arnaud

One of the most unusual of Mike Anderson's seafood recipes features huge fried shrimp with their tails turned up to form a sort of basket, and sauced with succulent Crabmeat Etouffée. Although so much Redfish has been eaten in New Orleans and shipped out of the state that a temporary ban was levied on catching them. There are wonderful substitutes such as Red Snapper, Orange Ruffy and Mahi Mahi being served now. Crawfish Etouffée was the most well-known meal in Cajun country. Etouffée simply means "smothered," as in a spicy sauce of its own, incorporating the fat of the crawfish.

Wine Sauce for Fruit

uart red wine
range, sliced
mes, sliced
love
innamon sticks
up sugar

ing wine to a boil. Add all ingredients and stir for inute. Bring to a boil a second time. Turn heat nd let mixture cool 30 minutes. Strain and refrig- until needed.

Recipe by Arnaud's

Shrimp Norman
Sauced With Crabmeat Etouffée

Clean, devein and butterfly (slit down back and spread flat) jumbo shrimp (6 per person). Dip in flour, then in milk and egg batter, and then in seasoned corn flour (sold commercially as "Fish-Fri" or at health food stores). Fry immediately in a deep heavy pot in fresh hot oil at 375 degrees until they float up and turn golden. Do not over fry. Serve on individual plates with tails turned up and every other one facing in the opposite direction. Pour the thick Crabmeat Etouffée down the center, leaving the tails sticking out on each side.

Crabmeat Etouffée

¾ stick butter
¼ cup flour
¼ cup green onion, chopped
¼ cup bell pepper, chopped
¼ cup minced celery
1 cup chicken stock or water
¼ cup white wine
1 teaspoon minced garlic
¼ cup chopped parsley
1 tablespoon lemon juice
1 pint crabmeat
   salt and pepper to taste

Melt butter until bubbly around the edges. Put in the onions, bell pepper and celery and sauté until soft. A dash of olive oil in the butter will keep it from burning. Add the flour gradually and blend in well. Start to blend in the hot chicken stock or water and continue until you have a thick creamy consistency. Add the white wine, garlic, parsley, lemon juice and seasonings and continue to simmer until blended in. Add the crabmeat and simmer again until it is well seasoned and you have achieved the proper consistency for a thick sauce. This can be made a little thinner and served as a separate dish with hot fluffy rice.

Recipes by Bobby Potts
(version of Mike Anderson's Specialties)

The Caribbean Room at the Pontchartrain Hotel on St. Charles Avenue is slightly "uptown," both in location and in style. For a couple of generations, some of the finest food in New Orleans has been served there. It was an especially nice atmosphere for ladies luncheons and was famous for its "Mile High Ice Cream Pie." It is not too far from downtown and is directly on the St. Charles Avenue streetcar line.

If one continues on up St. Charles Avenue on the street car, or by other means, until it meets Carrollton Avenue where the Mississippi makes a right angle turn, one arrives at the River-bend area, and almost immediately discovers the classiest grill in town with a Greek Revival facade. Some of the waiters have served at The Camellia Grill since it opened in the 1940's. Harry S. Tervalon, Sr. in our picture taken by the streetcar line, has become a living legend. They still serve the same menu: the biggest omelets and the juiciest hamburgers possible, and pies with a meringue that won't quit.

Crabmeat Far Horizons

ounces fresh lump crabmeat
cup light cream
teaspoon prepared mustard
capers
pinch of salt
teaspoons melted butter
tablespoons Hollandaise Sauce
Italian bread crumbs

This is for 1 serving.

ombine all ingredients in a thick aluminum pan.
g to a slow boil. Add butter. When mixture starts to
ken, add Hollandaise Sauce. Fold lightly without
g spoons to avoid breaking the crabmeat lumps.
en the consistency is right, spoon into a coquille shell
erving dish. Sprinkle with bread crumbs. Dot with
ll lumps of butter. Place coquille into 350 degree
n for 5 minutes, or place under a broiler until golden.

Veal With Three Herb Sauce

unces white veal
hole water chestnuts
esh white mushrooms
unces unsalted butter
unce all purpose flour
unces Marsala wine
up chicken stock
esh dill, fresh basil, fresh thyme

elt butter in sauté pan. Lightly dust veal in flour and
é (1½ minutes each side). Add sliced mushrooms,
d water chestnuts and Marsala wine. Watch heat so
e will not flame. Add chicken stock and chopped
s (combined to make 1 teaspoonful), and cook for 3
utes. Serve with angel hair pasta. Makes 1 serving.

*Recipes by Executive Chef Louis Evans,
Caribbean Room in the Pontchartrain Hotel*

Trout Veronique

1 trout filet per person
1 cup white wine
½ cup rich Hollandaise Sauce (see page 12 for recipe)
8 seedless grapes

Poach trout in wine in pan small enough so the wine covers the trout. Poach 7 minutes. Remove trout, draining well, and place on an ovenproof serving plate. Reduce remaining liquid over a fast fire, down to 2 cooking spoonfuls of liquid. Add Hollandaise Sauce and stir briskly. Place grapes on trout, cover with sauce and glaze quickly in the broiler. Makes 1 serving.

Mile High Ice Cream Pie

1 pint each of vanilla, chocolate and peppermint
    ice cream
8 egg whites (room temperature)
½ teaspoon vanilla
¼ teaspoon cream of tartar
½ cup sugar

Put a layer of vanilla ice cream in the bottom of a cold pie shell. Next, layer chocolate and peppermint ice cream. Set in freezer while making meringue. Beat egg whites with cream of tartar until a soft peak forms. Gradually add sugar and vanilla, beating until stiff and glossy (sugar is dissolved). Cover ice cream with meringue and put under broiler for 30 seconds to 1 minute (golden brown). Freeze for several hours. Drizzle chocolate sauce over each serving. Serves 8-12.

Seafood Omelet

2 tablespoons chopped green onions
4 oysters
2 ounces lump crabmeat
1 ounce white wine
1 tablespoon oil
1 tablespoon butter
4 large shrimp
4 fresh mushrooms, sliced
1 ounce cream
3 eggs

Sauté green onions in butter. Add oysters, crabmeat, mushrooms and wine. Cook until dry, then add cream. Beat eggs until frothy. Preheat oil in omelet pan, add eggs and seafood. Season, roll omelet and cook until done. Serves 2.

Recipe by Bobby Potts

Creole families that lived in the Quarter had designed their homes to be built above their shops and places of business, and had walled hidden courtyards in the rear. They could close up their businesses and go down to the courtyard in the evening, sometimes for supper, and languish under the palms and shade trees as the sun set. Raised flower beds were held in by low brick walls, and the fragrance of jasmine and gardenias added to the rarified atmosphere of a sub-tropical climate. Sometimes an "alleyway" leads from the street back to the courtyard, protected by a wrought iron gate, and we are able to get just a glimpse of the courtyard at the end of it.

Crab Claws Provencale

12 ounces garlic butter
 1 pound crab claws
 6 tablespoons Herbsaint
   pinch of chopped parsley

Melt butter in a pan over low flame. Add claws, stir gently until hot. Add Herbsaint and flame. Add salt and pepper to taste. Place crab claws in each of 6 small round ramekins (shell up). Pour a little of the sauce in each ramekin. Sprinkle with chopped parsley and serve. Serves 6.

Courtbouillon Sauce

 1 can tomatoes, chopped
 2 onions, diced
 2 stalks celery, chopped
 1 bell pepper, diced
 1 small can V-8 juice
 ½ teaspoon basil
 1 small can mushrooms
 ¼ cup chopped parsley
   salt, lemon pepper, and cayenne pepper to taste

This is a poaching medium used in the same way as a clear courtbouillon, except that it is richer and a little thicker, but keep it light enough so that it doesn't overwhelm the fish. Cook tomatoes, add vegetables, salt and pepper and continue cooking until tender. Add V-8 juice while cooking and water as necessary. Add the mushrooms and parsley just before finishing. This sauce can also be used with fish filets.

Boiled Crawfish

3 pounds live crawfish
1 gallon courtbouillon (see recipe at left)

Purge crawfish in a tub of cold water (no salt). Re[ ] twice (changing water each time). Place courtbouillon i[ ] large pot and bring to a boil over high heat. Add craw[ ] and cook for 7 minutes. Remove and drain. Allow to c[ ] then peel. *(For use only in recipes requiring boiled crawfish)*

Crawfish Bourgeois

1½ pounds crawfish tails (cooked and drained)
1½ cups mayonnaise (see next page)
 1 cup green onions, chopped
 1 teaspoon chopped garlic
 4 drops Tabasco
 2 teaspoons Dijon mustard
 1 teaspoon Lea & Perrins sauce
   salt and pepper to taste
   cayenne (red) pepper to taste
 2 tablespoons red wine vinegar
 6 tomatoes, medium size
 1 bunch watercress
12 black olives

In mixing bowl, combine mayonnaise, green onio[ ] garlic, Tabasco, mustard, Lea & Perrins, salt, pepper [ ] cayenne. Add red wine vinegar. Blend. Add craw[ ] Mix gently. Refrigerate 10 minutes. Cut tomatoe[ ] half and scoop out insides. Fill tomatoes with craw[ ] mixture. Top with a black olive. Place 2 stuffed to[ ] toes on each of 6 salad plates. Garnish with a sr[ ] bunch of watercress and serve immediately.

Escargots En Casserole

36 snails, drained and rinsed
 9 ounces garlic butter (see next page)
12 ounce frozen sheet puff pastry (⅛" thick)
 1 egg, whipped

Place each snail in a snail pot or ramekin. Cover e[ ] snail with garlic butter. Allow puff pastry to defrost [ ] cut 36 circles (using a 2" pastry cutter). Cover e[ ] snail pot with the puff pastry, pressing the edge lig[ ] to adhere. Brush egg on all puff pastry. Bake in 4[ ] degree oven for 8 minutes or until golden brown.

Recipes by Arna[ ]

*ome restaurants are fortunate enough to have a courtyard where they can serve a colorful sum-
*ner luncheon. Bull's Corner is one of these, and they have spread a meal of typically New
*Orleans-style dishes with a few country dishes such as "Panéed Veal" (flattened and breaded
*anfried veal), and very hot Lutcher Sausage shipped down from the town of Lutcher, Louisiana.

Mayonnaise

gg yolks
up Dijon mustard
alt and white pepper to taste
ups salad oil
ablespoon lemon juice

sing mixer, whip egg yolks, mustard, salt and pep-
or 3 minutes on low speed. Decrease speed and add
on juice. Check seasoning. Yields 1 quart.

Red Snapper Courtbouillon

¼ cup toasted bread cubes
4 tablespoons butter
6 chopped green onions
1 stalk celery, chopped
1 tablespoon chopped parsley
½ cup crabmeat
¼ cup white wine
½ cup mushrooms, chopped
½ teaspoon basil
   salt and pepper to taste

Moisten bread cubes with a little boiling water. Mix well with the melted butter in which all the chopped vegetables have been sautéed; include the seasonings, crabmeat and wine. Place cleaned fish in a baking dish. Head is usually left on. Rub outside of fish with butter. Season with salt and pepper. Stuff fish and fasten cavity closed. Pour the Courtbouillon Sauce (see recipe-opposite page) around it in the dish. Poach fish in the sauce for about 30 minutes in a 350 degree oven. Baste occasionally with the juice, adding more liquid as needed. Red wine may also be added to sauce. (Some chefs prefer to bake filets in the Courtbouillon rather than the whole fish.) *Courtbouillon is pronounced Coor-boo-yon.*

Garlic Butter

1 pound butter
¼ cup garlic, chopped finely
¼ cup parsley, chopped finely
4 tablespoons Herbsaint
   salt and pepper to taste

Using mixer at low speed, add butter and mix until soft. Add remaining ingredients and blend until mixture is soft enough to spread.

Recipes by Arnaud's

A jazz brunch is a tradition at the Court of Two Sisters. The balloons lend a festive air to the shady courtyard, and the buffet inside is luscious. One of the many New Orleans jazz bands will come in to put the finishing touch on helping you wake up with a hearty breakfast, so you will be ready to walk the streets of the Quarter and have many memories to take home with you.

Strawberry Omelet Cassis

Three egg omelet with ½ dozen sliced or whole strawberries folded in. After transferring to plate, top with a few more strawberries and shake several dashes of Cassis over omelet.

Marchand De Vin Sauce
(Wine Merchant Sauce)

¾ cup butter
½ cup ham
½ cup finely chopped onions
1 tablespoon flour
1 teaspoon white pepper
¾ cup beef stock
¾ cup finely chopped mushrooms
⅓ cup finely chopped shallots
2 tablespoons minced garlic
1 teaspoon salt
½ teaspoon cayenne pepper
½ cup red wine

Melt butter in medium saucepan. Lightly sauté mushrooms, ham, shallots, onions and garlic. When onion is golden brown, add flour, salt, pepper and cayenne, then brown well (7-10 minutes). Blend in the stock and wine and simmer on low heat for 35 minutes. Use with eggs, steak, chicken, etc.

Recipe by Brennan's

Shrimp Toulouse

¼ pound butter
½ cup chopped green onions
½ cup diced green peppers
¼ cup diced pimentos
¼ cup finely chopped celery
¼ cup chopped parsley
1 cup sliced mushrooms
3 pounds raw shrimp, peeled and deveined
1 cup white wine
6 patty shells

Melt butter, add sweet green pepper, green onions, celery, pimento, mushrooms and shrimp. Let simmer for 15 minutes. Add wine, salt and pepper to taste and simmer another 5 minutes. Add parsley and serve over a patty shell. Dust with paprika.

Recipes by Court of Two Sisters

Shrimp A La Fein

10 raw shrimp
2 strips bacon
2 green onions
  juice of 1 lemon
  salt and pepper to taste
1 tablespoon butter
  Tabasco
  Worcestershire Sauce
  paprika

Dice bacon and sauté in skillet until half coo[k] Pour off excess fat. Lower flame. Add butter, pe[el] raw shrimp, green onions chopped fine, and sea[son] to taste with salt and pepper. When shrimp are t[urn]ing pink, add lemon juice and a couple of dashes [each] of Tabasco and Worcestershire Sauce. Serve on t[oast] and dust with paprika. Makes 1 serving.

Eggs Hussarde

2 thin slices Canadian Bacon, grilled
¼ cup Marchand de Vin Sauce (see above)
2 poached eggs
2 Holland Rusks
1 grilled tomato
¼ cup Hollandaise Sauce (see page 12)

On a dinner plate, lay slices of Canadian Baco[n] 2 Holland Rusks, then cover each with Marchan[d de] Vin Sauce. Now top each rusk with a poached [egg] and cover all with the Hollandaise Sauce. Gar[nish] with grilled tomato. Sprinkle paprika and cho[pped] parsley on eggs.

s the band plays good old New Orleans jazz like it is played nowhere else in the world, good
rong coffee is served and you can meander inside to the long buffet tables where more differ-
t things are offered than you thought could be possible for breakfast. But this isn't just
eakfast. It is a hearty brunch from a heavily laden board, and you may not be hungry
ain all day.

Shrimp Creole

nd butter
 chopped sweet onions
 chopped green onions
 tomato purée or two tablespoons tomato paste
ice lemon juice
ices cornstarch
 chopped green bell peppers
 diced celery
s chopped canned tomatoes
 leaves
inds peeled and deveined shrimp
ck or cayenne pepper to taste
 to taste

lt butter, sauté pepper, onion, celery and shal-
or 5 minutes. Add tomato purée or paste, bay
s, and simmer 15 minutes. Add shrimp and
er 15 minutes. Dissolve cornstarch in one pint
iter, add and simmer 5 minutes. Add lemon
salt and pepper to taste, and a pinch of cayenne
i desire. Simmer another 15 minutes. Serve
ing hot over a bed of white long grain rice.

Stuffed Pork Chops

8 pork chops
3 cups bread cubes
¼ diced celery, sautéed lightly
1 cup chopped oysters
½ cup oysters liquor
1 cup diced onions
1 cup crabmeat
2 eggs
 salt and pepper to taste

Combine all dry ingredients with crabmeat, oysters
and eggs. Mix as you would any bread stuffing. Place
about 1 cup of stuffing between 2 pork chops and
bake in a greased baking pan. Bake at 350 degrees for
25-30 minutes. Serve with a brown sauce.

Recipes by Court of Two Sisters

Shrimp Mousse

1 8 ounce package cream cheese
1 can tomato soup
1 tablespoon unflavored gelatin
½ cup water
1 cup mayonnaise
2 tablespoons lemon juice
2 tablespoons chopped green onions
2 cups chopped shrimp
½ teaspoon paprika
 salt and pepper
 dash of Tabasco
2 tablespoons horseradish

Melt cream cheese in hot soup. Blend well. Add
slowly to gelatin that has been dissolved in water.
Stir all other ingredients into cooled mixture and pour
into mold that has been greased with mayonnaise.
Refrigerate at least 6 hours, preferably overnight.
Loosen edge gently with knife, cover with serving
plate, and invert. Garnish with parsley. (Made without shrimp or other seafood, this is a good substitute
for tomato aspic, especially with sliced pimento olives
and chopped pecans added to it.)

Recipe by Bobby Potts

There are so many different seafoods available in New Orleans and so many different ways serve them, that the varieties never seem to run out. Oysters baked on the half shell give good example. The original dish of this sort was Oysters Rockefeller, covered with a sauce spinach and greens flavored with absinthe and baked on a pan of rock salt to hold the hea Then along came Oysters Bienville, baked with a cheesy cream sauce, which has now bee around for a long time. In addition, most restaurants have their own special baked oyste covered with their steaming "house" sauce. Usually you can order 2-2-2 oysters, whic means, 2 Rockefeller, 2 Bienville, and 2 "House," whatever it may be.

Oysters Rockefeller

Rockefeller Sauce

1 cup oyster water
¼ bunch green onions, chopped
½ cup plain bread crumbs
¼ bunch spinach
2 stalks celery, finely minced
1 cup plain water
1 sprig thyme, chopped
1 ounce Herbsaint or Pernod
1 cup butter
1 teaspoon anchovy paste
1 tablespoon Worcestershire Sauce

Procure fresh oysters on the half shell, save the oyster water from them, and then wash and drain the shells. Now put the oysters back in their shells. Place coarse ice cream salt to the thickness of about ½" in an oven proof baking dish or metal pan and preheat. Place the oysters on the half shells on top of the hot salt and run them in the broiler for about 5 minutes, until they curl. Then cover with the Rockefeller Sauce and bread crumbs and bake in a hot oven until brown. Serve very hot. Yields 2 dozen.

Oysters En Brochette

2 dozen raw oysters
4 eight inch skewers
¾ cup milk
   salt and pepper to taste
12 strips bacon, cut in half
1 egg
   flour
   oil for deep frying

Fry bacon until not quite crisp. Alternate 6 oysters and 6 half strips of back (folded) on each skewer. Make a batter with egg and milk. Season well with salt and pepper. Dip each skewer in batter, roll in flour and deep fry until golden. Serve on toast points with lemon wedge. Serves 4 as an appetizer or 2 as a main course.

Recipes by Bobby Potts

Oysters Bienville

Bienville Sauce

4 strips bacon
⅓ cup sliced fresh mushrooms
2 cloves garlic, chopped
3 tablespoons butter
¼ cup chopped green onions
1 quart hot milk
⅔ cup oyster juice
⅓ cup sherry wine
⅓ cup fresh lemon juice
¼ cup chopped parsley
⅔ cup flour
⅓ pound boiled shrimp, chopped

Cut bacon into small pieces. Fry until brown. mushrooms, garlic and shallots and cook until s minutes). Add butter to pan, stirring until m Blend in flour and cook for 5 minutes. Graduall hot milk and stir until thick and smooth. Ac shrimp, oyster juice, lemon juice, sherry and pa Cook over low heat for 15 minutes and top the ters with this mixture before baking in the oven

Broil 4 dozen oysters in the half shell for minutes until they curl slightly. Then cover oyster with Bienville Sauce. Bake in a hot over degrees, until the top is brown and crisp.

Recipe by Commander's

OYSTER BARS: INTEGRAL PART OF NEW ORLEANS

For aficionados, raw oysters are tantalizing for the palate. They are judged by their saltiness and texture, and the partaker usually prefers to stand at the bar and eat them off the half shell, mixing his own sauce for dipping from the condiments placed on the bar, such as catsup, horseradish, hot sauce, lemon juice, and whatever else he craves. Felix's and Acme Oyster Bars are typical with the waiters opening the oysters fresh and placing them on a bed of ice to be eaten immediately while they are fresh.

Basic Cocktail Sauce for Oysters

1 cup ketchup
1 tablespoon horseradish
　Tabasco Sauce to taste
1 tablespoon lemon juice
1 tablespoon tarragon vinegar
1 tablespoon Worcestershire Sauce

Mix all the ingredients until they are perfectly blended. Taste and see if it suits you. There are other ingredients that can be used or added depending upon your taste. Possibilities are Pickapeppa Sauce, Cajun Power Garlic Sauce, Cajun Power Herb Sauce, Cream of Horseradish or if you have a garden, you can have freshly ground horseradish (which is really hot), and you can make your own tarragon vinegar or other herb vinegars. Some even like a touch of sugar in it. Make it ahead and chill it for at least a day. You can make it in quantity and keep it on hand for several weeks because of all the hot seasonings. Use on shrimp, crabs, crawfish or flaked fish in addition to oysters.

Broiled Crabmeat, Oysters, Scallops and Softshelled Crabs

you like broiled seafood, try broiling crabmeat, ers, scallops and softshelled crabs or other seafood is simple method. For each serving, use 4 tablens butter, 1 teaspoon lemon juice and a couple of es of Worcestershire Sauce in a pan. Sauté the meat (5-8 minutes), oysters (until edges are curled), ps (15 minutes) or softshelled crabs (7 minutes on side) until almost done. Finish each under the r, in the oven, or in the pan itself. Serve with the n butter sauce from the pan. They could even be d together as a mixed grill is served.

Bucktown is an old section of New Orleans at the far end of Lake Ponchartrain. It used to have a string of little shacks along the water front, and years ago we would drive out there just to see what the whole little village looked like. The people would peer out at us very suspiciously, which made us feel that we should not linger. That has all changed now, and there is a residential area not far from the water. Bucktown is now the place to go for seafood. Deanie's has built a great reputation for having an abundance of boiled seafood, although they have fried seafood, too. ♠ People in Louisiana have always had a fondness for boiled seafood. Whether at a family picnic or at a restaurant, they love to sit down to a huge pile of crabs, shrimp, or crawfish and eat them as they peel them. They taste so fresh that way because they are plump and moist and delicious. It is remarkable to see the amount that some people can eat as they just sit and peel and pop them in their mouths. Crisp little filets of fried catfish are popular here, too, as are the various kinds of po'boy sandwich loaves stuffed with fried oysters, shrimp or catfish.

Stuffed Shrimp

6 large onions, chopped
6 stems of celery, minced
2 bell peppers, chopped
2 cloves garlic, minced
½ cup cooking oil
1 pound raw shrimp, chopped
  salt and pepper to taste
2 cups day old bread, torn up
1 pound white lump crabmeat
1 tablespoon chopped parsley
2 eggs, beaten lightly
4 pounds large shrimp

Chop onions, pepper, celery and garlic. Sauté in oil until tender. Add chopped raw shrimp, salt and pepper. Cook until the shrimp are done. Toast the day old bread and soak in water to moisten. Squeeze out water and add bread to mixture, a little at a time, mixing well. Add crabmeat and parsley. Let cook for 5 minutes. Set aside to cool. Add raw egg. While mixture is cooling, peel and devein shrimp, leaving on the tail shell. Take a small sharp knife and split down the back, making sure not to cut completely through the shrimp. Fill the backs of the shrimp with dressing, then freeze. When ready to cook, dip shrimp in flour, then in beaten egg and milk, and then in the flour again. Fry in deep hot oil at 350 degrees.

Recipe by Pascal's Manale

Boiled Crabs

28 ounces of salt
64 ounces Chinese peppers
½ gallon liquid crab boil
16 ounces garlic powder
32 ounces lemon juice
2 hampers raw crabs

Bring water to a boil. Add seasoning. Place crabs in water. Let water come back to the boil stage; then boil 10 minutes. Turn fire off. Put ice in pot to stop boiling. Let crabs soak in seasoning for 20 minutes.

Recipe by Deanie's

...ed Fantail Shrimp in Beer Batter

...p sifted flour
...spoon each of sugar and salt
...sh pepper
...sh nutmeg
...spoon baking powder
...aten egg
...p beer
...unds fresh shrimp
...oking oil for frying

...ork above ingredients, except for shrimp, into a ...batter. Peel shell from shrimp, leaving the last sec-...and tail intact. Cut almost through at the center ...without cutting the ends. Dry shrimp and dip into ...batter. Fry in deep, hot fat until golden brown. ... and serve at once.

Recipe by Bobby Potts

Boiled Shrimp

20 ounces Worcestershire Sauce
32 ounces garlic powder
½ gallon corn oil
96 ounces salt
48 ounces Chinese peppers
½ gallon liquid crab boil
32 ounces lemon juice
50 pounds raw shrimp

Let water come to a boil. Add all seasoning. Place shrimp in pot. Once water comes back to a boiling stage, boil shrimp 2-3 minutes. Turn fire off. Put ice in it to stop boiling, but let shrimp soak in seasoning another 20 minutes.

Recipe by Deanie's

33

Seafood in Louisiana is most commonly fried, but it is also baked and broiled. Especial, since everyone is watching their diets, we now eat more baked and broiled seafood than w used to. However, we do not commonly see steamed seafood, but it is delicious because retains all of its flavor and comes to the table fresh and moist. Vicko's, across the River, famous for their steamed seafood.

Steamed Red Snapper

1 red or yellow bell pepper
6 green onions with tender parts of the green tops
2 stalks celery, chopped very fine
1 tablespoon butter or margarine
 tarragon, salt and pepper to taste
4 red snapper filets, 6-8 ounces
 dash of white wine and 1 of lemon juice

Melt the butter and sauté all of the vegetables until soft. Add the tarragon, and salt and pepper to taste. Use a steamer basket or place a flat bottomed colander over a pot full of steaming water. Lay the fish in it and steam for 7-8 minutes until just done.

Do not overcook the fish. Place the fish on ser plates with the vegetables around it or over the Sprinkle the wine and lemon juice lightly over top and serve immediately (or serve with a lemon wedge).

Shrimp and crawfish can be steamed in the s way, but watch carefully because they cook quite There is also a way to steam seafood in microwave. Wet a paper towel with lightly run water from the faucet. Place it on a plate with the soned seafood in the center of it, bring the 4 corner to cover it, and put it in the microwave for abo minutes. Then return it, a minute at a time, until done the way you want it. Then garnish and serve

In the northern part of the United States, children are known to hunt for "crayfish" in the ponds, and they come up with little brown mudbugs that aren't of much use for anything. But in the warmer climates of the south, the mudbugs grow to a very large size and the Cajun people call them "crawfish." When we hear someone call them crayfish, we think they are putting on airs, so we would never let anyone catch us calling them crayfish. Just as we would never let anyone hear us say shrimps when there are more than one, as they do up north. In New Orleans, we say "shrimp," whether singular or plural.

Crawfish Pies

pound crawfish, coarsely ground
  (save the yellow crawfish fat)
up butter or margarine
up each of bell pepper, parsley, and celery
up chopped green onions
an stewed tomatoes
up creamy onion soup, or make your own
hopped boiled eggs
ablespoon Teriyaki Sauce
up seasoned bread crumbs
alt and cayenne pepper to taste

is important to chop all vegetables very finely. pies are small and the ingredients should blend ether well. Sauté them in the butter and mix the vfish in when they are soft. If you peel the craw- yourself, it is important to save the fat as it adds atly to the taste. Run the tomatoes through a food cessor, add to the mixture and simmer for 20 min- s until somewhat reduced. Add the soup or cream ce, stirring well, add the chopped eggs and heat a e longer. It should have a nice thick creamy con- ency. If it is too thick, add a little milk or water. nove from the fire and stir in the bread crumbs. l liquid again if necessary. Spoon into unbaked shells and bake in a 350 degree oven until wned, about 30 minutes. Makes 16 small tarts.

Cream of Crawfish Soup

1 pound crawfish, cleaned
1 small carrot and small onion
2 sprigs parsley
  water
½ teaspoon thyme
1 cup white wine
1 bay leaf
2 tablespoons butter
1 green onion, minced
2 tablespoons minced celery
1 tablespoon minced parsley
1 small tomato, diced fine
1 tablespoon flour
2 cups light cream
  salt and pepper to taste
  Finish with ¼ cup of Madeira, Sherry, or Brandy

Poach crawfish in simmering pot of water (enough to cover the crawfish with chopped up carrot, onion, and some parsley). Add thyme, wine and bay leaf. Continue to simmer for about 10 minutes. Remove shrimp, peel, devein and chop the meat fine. Strain liquid and reserve.

Melt butter in a stew pan, sauté onion and celery until clear. Lower heat. Add parsley and tomato and cook down a little. Add flour and cream it into butter. Heat until golden. Slowly pour the hot, strained shrimp stock back into the roux and blend in as you add. Pour cream in, add salt and white pepper. Simmer until it is the consistency of a proper cream sauce. Add the Madeira when ready to serve. Top with a pat of butter and a sprig of parsley. If serving later, be sure to bring it to a boil before serving.

Recipe by Chef Patty Rives

There are many small neighborhood restaurants about town that are not well known to travelers coming to New Orleans, but many of them are excellent. Some are places where local business men may meet for lunch, and some are more family oriented. They are not usually stylish restaurants, but thrive on just plain well-cooked food. A few, however, have specialties of the house that could well be classified as gourmet, especially for the uninitiated.

Red Snapper with Crawfish Tails

Allow 1 eight to ten-ounce Red Snapper filet for each person. Season and lightly flour the filets and sauté for 7-8 minutes (4 minutes on each side with hot oil).

1 bunch green onions, chopped (save green tops)
½ glass red wine
¼ cup heavy cream
1 stick butter
½ teaspoon thyme
   salt and white pepper

Crawfish Tail Sauce:

½ pound tails
   green onion tops, chopped
1 clove garlic, minced
1 teaspoon butter
1 tablespoon white wine
   salt and pepper

In a separate small skillet, sauté the green onion tops and garlic in butter for 2 minutes. Add the crawfish tails and the salt and pepper and sauté 2 minutes more. Add white wine and sauté 30 seconds more.

Make a Beurre Rouge (red butter) sauce, using a small saucepan and boil the white parts of the green onions in the red wine. Reduce by ½. Add cream and boil 2-3 minutes longer until it starts to thicken. Add thyme and turn down to a low simmer. Gradually add the butter, whisking constantly until all of it is incorporated into the sauce. Keep the sauce at room temperature. It breaks down at temperatures of over 100 degrees.

Sauce bottom of each plate with Beurre Rouge Sauce. Lay the broiled Red Snapper filet in center of plate, and ladle the hot crawfish across the middle of it from side to side. Garnish with a sprig of fresh rosemary or parsley.

Recipe by Chef Parker Murphy

Shrimp Salad

1 cup cooked, chopped shrimp
2 hard-boiled eggs, chopped
¼ cup celery, minced
¼ cup scallions, chopped
¼ cup parsley, chopped
½ cup chopped cucumber
2 tablespoons minced bell pepper
4 tablespoons mayonnaise
2 teaspoons hot sweet mustard
   lemon-pepper and salt to taste

Toss all the dry ingredients. Mix in the season Blend the mustard into the mayonnaise and st into the salad. This recipe may be used for crabm or any other cold seafood. Serve on a bed of let with a lemon wedge.

Grilled Shrimp

½ cup salad oil
   juice of 1 lemon
½ cup white wine
⅛ cup herb or soy sauce
1 tablespoon brown sugar
   salt and pepper to taste

Mix ingredients thoroughly. Marinate some large shrimp while the coals are heating up in grill. Lay them on a screen or fine grill so they not fall through. Turn and baste on both sides done. It won't take long.

Nouvelle Cajun and Creole sounds like a contradiction in terms, since both are very traditional cuisines, and especially since we think of both Cajun and Creole as being very rich and high in calories, and since Nouvelle Cuisine is considered to be leaner fare for the diet conscious. However, Flagon's restaurant in the Irish Channel area has developed a lighter, leaner menu based on traditional tastes of Louisiana. It is a wine bar with a clientele that appreciates the kind of gourmet cooking that doesn't ruin the waistline.

Shrimp with Ginger and Garlic Sauce

large shrimp per person
cups oil
tablespoons garlic, minced
tablespoon green onions, minced
teaspoon sesame oil
ounces catsup
ounces chicken stock
salt and pepper to taste

Heat oil in skillet. Add shrimp that have been butterflied and stir fry until just pink. Remove. Drain all but 3 tablespoons of oil. Add ginger, garlic and green onions. Sauté until they are golden. Add shrimp and catsup. Thin with stock and reduce sauce over medium high heat. Season with salt, pepper and Tabasco if desired. Serve over hot rice.

Recipes by Flagon's

Shrimp and Tasso Pasta

4 dozen large shrimp
4 bamboo skewers
1 cup vegetable oil
4 tablespoons minced garlic
  salt and pepper to taste

Peel shrimp but leave tail on. Thread 12 shrimp to a skewer. Marinate in oil, garlic, and a generous amount of salt and pepper for at least 4 hours.

1 pound fettucine noodles, drained
1 ounce butter
6 ounces Tasso or smoked ham, diced
1 teaspoon garlic, minced, cooked
1 tablespoon scallions, minced
12 ounces heavy cream
3 ounces grated Parmesan cheese
  salt and pepper to taste

Melt butter in a large skillet. Add tasso, garlic and scallions. Sauté 1 minute. Add cream and cook over medium heat until reduced by ⅓. Stir in Parmesan cheese and seasonings. Add cooked fettucine and toss well.

Broil or grill skewered shrimp, turning to brown on all sides. Place hot pasta on each plate. Position the skewer across the top of the pasta and gently withdraw the skewer, holding the shrimp in place as you do it. Grill quarters of onions, tomatoes and bell pepper while you are doing the shrimp, and serve them on the side of the plate with lemon wedges.

Note: Tasso is often called Cajun Jerky. It is smoked dry and hotly seasoned and is often used in cooking vegetables for seasoning. You could probably substitute pieces of hotly seasoned beef jerky if you cannot find tasso, but it is now available in other cities.

The Faubourgs were the first "subdivisions" that were built outside of the French Quarter. The first ones were built along the Riverfront just downriver from the Quarter. Today they are quiet old neighborhoods with picturesque small houses and unpretentious business establishments. Feeling's Cafe D'Aunoy is in Faubourg Marigny, adjacent to the Quarter, and it has been discovered by many of the people from "uptown" who come for good food and quiet conversation. This land was originally a large plantation owned by Nicholas d'Aunoy. There is an upstairs room and a balcony that looks over the courtyard. It is a peaceful place where one can catch a breath of air in the evening. La Peniche is another of these neighborhood restaurants in the Faubourg, which has a great following of people who find it a comfortable spot in which to dine.

Seafood Thermidor

4 ounces butter or margarine
2 green onions, minced
2 tablespoons flour
2 cups seafood stock (or chicken stock)
2 tablespoons white wine
   salt and pepper to taste
1 pound each of peeled shrimp, crawfish
     and cubed redfish
   parsley for garnish

Melt butter in saucepan, add onions. Sauté until tender. Add flour. Blend into a smooth white roux. Cook over low heat and do not brown. Add stock and wine slowly and stir until well blended. Let simmer 10 minutes. Salt and pepper to taste. Sauté shrimp, crawfish and redfish in large sauté pan. Stir in Thermidor Sauce.

Recipe by Feeling's Café D'Aunoy

Avacado Dressing

1 mashed ripe avocado
1½ cup mayonnaise
1 lemon, juice only
1 clove garlic, chopped
1 teaspoon salt
1 teaspoon crushed black pepper
½ teaspoon anchovy paste
1 cup whipping cream

Mix well and refrigerate.

Salad dressing recipes by Le Ruth's

Sweet and Sour Celery Seed Dressing

3 tablespoons catsup
2 tablespoons white vinegar
1 tablespoon sugar
¼ teaspoon salt
¼ cup light corn syrup
2 teaspoons steak sauce
2 tablespoons water
1 teaspoon onion juice
1 teaspoon whole celery seeds
3 tablespoons corn oil

Mix well and refrigerate.

Roquefort Dressing

1 cup mayonnaise
2 tablespoons sour cream
2 tablespoons buttermilk
¼ teaspoon Lea & Perrins
¼ teaspoon white pepper
⅛ teaspoon M.S.G.
½ teaspoon salt
2-3 ounces Roquefort cheese, crumbled

Mix well and refrigerate.

Russian Dressing

⅔ cup mayonnaise
⅓ cup chili sauce
1½ tablespoons finely chopped green bell pepper
1 tablespoon each chopped pimento and onion
1 tablespoon each of sugar and vinegar
¼ teaspoon Lea & Perrins

Mix well and refrigerate.

he Le Ruth family is famous for its ability to cook the best food ever. Warren Le Ruth found-
d a restaurant in Gretna that is no longer in existence, but his two sons Lee and Larry stud-
d abroad to become great chefs. In addition to their ability to prepare excellent meat and
eafood, they also make wonderful desserts and breads. They allowed us to photograph the
rocess of bread making in their kitchen.

Covington Pear Bread

ips sugar
ggs
ip salad oil
iblespoon salt
aspoon grated orange rind
ips grated raw pears
unces liqueur (Southern Comfort)
ips all purpose flour
aspoon baking soda
aspoon baking powder
aspoon vanilla
ip chopped pecans

x sugar and eggs, add oil, salt, orange rind and
. Stir in liqueur, vanilla and dry ingredients. Stir
is last. Bake in greased loaf pan in 350 degree
for 45 minutes.

Chocolate Comfort Pie
(Pecan Pie with Chocolate)

4 whole eggs
1 teaspoon vanilla
1¼ cups brown sugar
1¼ cups light Karo syrup
2 ounces Southern Comfort
1½ cups pecans (chopped or whole, as preferred)

Beat together all of the above ingredients. On the
side, melt 1 stick of butter and ½ cup chocolate chips,
stirring carefully so as not to burn. Add to first mixture. Bake in regular pie dough.

Recipes by Le Ruth's

Lee Making the Daily Supply of French Bread

Lee says Larry makes the best
bread, but Lee showed us the
process. They use straight dough
only. No sour dough, so there is
no "punching down" to be done.
The ingredients for the bread
dough first go into a huge mixer.
After being thoroughly mixed, it is
taken out and lightly rolled. The
baker then cuts chunks of dough
off and literally throws them into
the top of the sheeter. The sheeter
flattens the dough. Then it hits the
chains that roll the dough up into a
long "sausage" shape which pops
out on the bread pan. About 8
loaves are placed on each sheet. It
is then put in the proofer, which
steams the bread. After that, it is
ready for baking.

One can take the ferry or the bridge to the other side of the river and view the night skyline of New Orleans from the Algiers side of the river. At Algiers Landing, we sat and watched as the sun went down behind us and the night lights gradually turned on as the sky darkened.

Chicken Fricassée

A longtime favorite in the homes of New Orleans.

1 chicken (about 4 pounds), cut up
  seasoned flour
1 tablespoon shortening
1 chopped onion
1 sprig thyme
1 tablespoon minced parsley
1 bay leaf
3 cups boiling water

Mix salt and pepper in with enough flour to coat the chicken. When well coated, brown the chicken pieces in the hot shortening. (Egg is not used in this recipe because batter would not do well.) Add the onions and sauté. Add herbs and water. Bring to a rolling boil, then cover and reduce heat. Simmer until tender (about one hour). Serves 8.

Tournedos

2 tablespoons butter
½ cup sliced mushrooms
1 tablespoon flour
½ cup mushroom juice
¼ cup red wine
¼ cup Worcestershire Sauce
¼ teaspoon salt
  a dash of cayenne (red) pepper
4 small filets mignon
1 large ripe tomato

In a small saucepan, melt butter and sauté mushrooms. Add flour and cook slowly a few minutes until slightly browned. Stir in wine, mushroom juice and seasonings. Cook until thickened. While this is cooking, season and grill filets to taste (rare or medium rare). Cut the tomato into 4 nice slices and grill. Arrange tomato slice on each filet and pour mushroom sauce over all.

Boeuf Wellington

I am sure Wellington did not call it boeuf, but th what it is called in New Orleans restaurants.

42 ounce beef tenderloin
4 ounces goose liver, sliced
1 pound puff pastry
1 ounce truffles
1 pound fresh mushrooms, chopped (or ½ pound canned mushrooms)

Roast the beef tenderloin approximately 10 minutes in the oven for medium rare. Put the r back into the refrigerator and chill until cold. Ro of the puff pastry approximately ¼" thick until 1½ times the dimension of the beef. Sauté chopped mushrooms in butter and spread on the pastry. On top of the mushrooms, place the b Place goose liver over the beef and then the truf Roll the puff pastry into a mound and close with mixture (1 egg mixed with salt, and beaten). egg mixture is used like glue and is applied wit brush. With the remainder of the pastry, mak design on the top. Put the Boeuf Wellington o tray and place in the refrigerator for 15 minu Then place it in the oven for 20 minutes at appr mately 400 degrees. Serve after 20 minutes wi Bearnaise Sauce (see page 6). If you do not s immediately, the beef will continue to cook from steam in the pastry shell. Serves 6.

They prepare food in Algiers, across the river, that is just as spicy and flavorful as in New Orleans. The traditions have been spread all around the area on both sides and up and down the river, but everyone gives the food their own special touch. However, the excellent seasoning, complete with herbs and a dash of cayenne pepper, is to be found everywhere.

Escargots Bordelaise

rocure canned snails and packaged snail shells at r market. Allow at least 6 per person. Wash shells snails and place 6 shells in a small plate for each on. Use oven proof plates, preferably those made cially for snails with small concave spaces to put shells in, or bake in a baking dish and transfer . This recipe will do for 4 dozen snails.

lix 1 finely chopped large onion, 2 minced cloves garlic, 2 tablespoons finely chopped parsley, a h of tarragon, 1 teaspoon salt and ½ teaspoon k pepper into 1 cup soft butter, smoothing it all ther and blending it well.

a sauté pan, stir 2 tablespoons flour into 2 table- ons melted butter and brown, but do not burn, ing more butter if necessary. Then stir red deaux wine in gradually until you have a sauce of ce consistency. Pour a little of the sauce into each l, place a snail in each shell and seal with some of butter mixture. Bake in a hot oven for 10-15 utes until they are browning and bubbly. Serve

hot with small pieces of French Bread. It is de rigeur to mop up the sauce with the bread because it is far too tasty to waste.

Chicken Bonne Femme

2 chickens cut up for frying
½ cup oil
4 potatoes, sliced thin
1 large onion, sliced
1 clove garlic, minced
  salt to taste
  cayenne (red) pepper to taste
¼ cup chopped parsley

Sauté chicken in oil until done and lightly browned. Sprinkle seasoning on chicken while it is cooking. As soon as you begin to fry the chicken, cottage fry the potatoes. After they are done, drain all the oil from the pan of chicken, place it in a serving dish, and top with the potatoes and parsley.

Many immigrants came from Italy to settle in or near the French Quarter. Some became truck farmers in the nearby countryside or in Algiers and brought their produce to the French Market. Others opened restaurants, shops and bakeries. They have had a great influence on the Quarter and good Italian food has always been here. ♠ In the Central Grocery Store on Decatur Street, one finds a most authentic Italian Grocery Store. Garlic is hung from the ceiling, sausages and cheeses tied up with heavy twine are displayed on the counter, and a wonderful assortment of the best olive oils are to be found on the shelf. In another part of the store, bins are stocked with huge variety of pasta. Best of all, there is a wide counter where Muffaletta sandwiches are literally built for you on white butcher paper. Then you may carry your sandwich on its butcher paper to small tables or a marble counter to eat it.

Bolognese Sauce

This is the rich red sauce that can be used on any pasta dish, or on Lasagna, Beef Roll-ups, or Canneloni.

¼ cup olive oil
1 six-ounce can tomato paste
1 large onion, chopped fine
2 cloves garlic, minced
3 medium carrots, chopped fine
2 celery stalks, chopped fine
2 cans Italian plum tomatoes
1 can tomato purée
¼ cup of your favorite rich beef sauce
    (I prefer A-1 or a Sauce Diable)
2 teaspoons crushed sweet basil
1 teaspoon oregano
1 can beef stock
  salt and pepper and sugar to taste
1 tablespoon Balsamic Vinegar
  Your preference in wine: Marsala, Dry Sherry,
    or Burgundy

Heat the oil and add the can of tomato paste, smoothing it gradually into the oil. Brown it slightly. This takes away that "tinny" taste that it tends to have. Add the chopped vegetables and more oil if necessary and let them cook alone a little before adding all the vegetables with the plum tomatoes and tomato purée. Let them cook down a little and then add the beef sauce and the herbs. Add the beef stock gradually and let it continue to thicken. You do not want this to be a watery sauce. Add the salt and pepper and then play with the sugar and vinegar, adding a little of each at a time to balance each other and then tasting it. The sugar makes everything blend together, but you don't really want it to taste sweet. Add the wine last. Marsala is very Italian, of course, but I prefer Burgundy in the heavy rich sauce. I save the Marsala for Chicken Marsala with herbs and brown gravy.

Recipe by Bobby Potts

Muffalettas

The only way I can tell you how to make a Muffaletta Italian sandwich is to send you to your nearest Italian market. Buy all the different kinds of Bologna and Italian Sausage that can be sliced for a sandwich but only as much as you think you can eat. The same instructions follow for the wonderful Italian cheeses, Mozzarella, Provalone, Romano and so forth. Then get a large round loaf of Italian bread and some fresh Italian chopped up olive salad, or buy it in a jar. Now go home and go to work. Slice the bread in half crosswise and layer in the meats and cheeses, alternating them if you like. Toss some of the salad olives across the top, and there you are. You may dress the sandwich any way you like; with butter, mayonnaise, or by lightly pouring a little olive oil over the bread to sort of lubricate it. There is no law that says you cannot put lettuce and tomatoes on it, but I think it will be better without. Now cut the big loaf across the top and then across again at right angles, which will give you 4 sandwiches, and most people can only eat one of them. If you want to make it really authentic, wrap each quarter in butcher paper, stick a toothpick in the top to hold the paper and pass them out. Have fun!

n equally fascinating Italian restaurant is Pascal's Manale's Restaurant in the uptown sec-
...on of New Orleans. The walls are hung with posters of famous opera singers, and one room
...as burgundy red wall paper which creates an atmosphere that makes your palate cry for
...alian food. They are most famous for their Barbecued Shrimp, and they definitely do not
...ive out their recipe for it, so I will try to do the best I can for you.

Barbecued Shrimp

8 pounds large shrimp, unpeeled
½ pound butter
1 cup olive oil
8 ounces chili sauce
3 tablespoons Teriyaki Sauce
2 lemons, sliced
4 cloves garlic
3 tablespoons lemon juice
1 small onion, diced
1 tablespoon parsley, chopped
2 teaspoons paprika
2 teaspoons oregano
2 teaspoons red pepper
1 teaspoon Tabasco Sauce
3 tablespoons liquid smoke
1 tablespoon brown sugar
3 tablespoons dry sherry
  salt to taste

Wash shrimp, spread out in a shallow pan. Combine ingredients in a sauce pan, simmer over low heat until everything is blended and vegetables are soft, and pour over shrimp. Refrigerate, baste and turn shrimp every 30 minutes over a period of a few hours. Bake at 300 degrees or panbroil for 30 minutes, and turn shrimp over every 10 minutes. Serve in a soup or pasta bowl with plenty of French Bread to dip into the sauce.

Recipes by Bobby Potts

Tira Mi Su (Pick-me-up)

...e the bottom and sides of a 9"x12" dish with dry lady fingers
...ge cake may also be used). Sprinkle strong coffee or coffee liqueur
... the bottom cookies, but don't soak. Spread a jar of soft (not liquid)
...olate over the bottom. Soften and cream a carton of Mascarpone
...se (Italian) and stir a small carton of Cool Whip or La Creme into it.
...n thoroughly mixed, spread all of it over the chocolate. Refrigerate.
...e serving, swirl or make a criss-cross pattern across the top with
...l chocolate sauce.

Toney's Spaghetti House is one of the traditional restaurants of New Orleans. They always stayed open late at night, and the show people of the Quarter could come there after their acts and have a late supper and friendly conversation before they went home to bed. They serve very typical Italian dishes, and it is a friendly place for a comfortable conversation.

Bracciolone

You will want enough heavy veal or young beef to have 2 pieces the size of a veal cutlet for each person. This is the Italian equivalent of our regular "Veal Birds" or Beef Roll-ups. Place the "Bracciole" (round of beef) between 2 pieces of wax paper and pound each carefully until it thins out, but do not break it. Sauté 1 medium onion, chopped, and ½ a chopped bell pepper in a little olive oil. Place them in a mixing bowl. Add ¼ cup parsley, and ½ cup Romano or Parmesan cheese, grated. Add 2 cloves of garlic minced, 1 raw egg, and a small amount of milk. Mix together until it becomes a thick paste that you can spread on the individual rounds, adding a little milk as necessary. Then spread it on and roll the rounds up tightly, securing with a toothpick. Brown the rolls in olive oil, place in a large baking dish, cover with a Bolognese Sauce and bake at 350 degrees for at least an hour to an 1½ hours.

There is a Middle Eastern influence in Italy and some like their meat with sweet flavors added, and they add raisins or pine nuts to the mixture. Chopped carrots and chopped ham may also be added to it. For a richer dish, browned ground meat can be added to it. There are many variations to this dish, so create your own. It is usually served with a Bolognese Sauce, but it could also be served with a brown gravy, especially the sweet kind.

Recipe by Bobby Potts

Stuffed Manicotti

1½ pounds ground beef
¼ cup minced onion
1 rib minced celery
3-4 cloves garlic
¼ cup Romano cheese
2 eggs
salt to taste
white pepper to taste
1 cup minced parsley
1 cup bread crumbs (may use seasoned crumbs

Brown meat and drain; sauté onion, garlic celery. Combine all ingredients; shape into saus like rolls and insert into cooked manicotti sh Place shells in a greased baking dish and p Bolognese Sauce over them. Bake at 350 deg for 25 to 30 minutes.

Shrimp Scallopine

3-4 tablespoons olive oil
2 medium bell peppers, sliced
1 medium onion, sliced
1½ teaspoons minced garlic
1 sixteen-ounce can whole tomatoes, drained and chopped
2 tablespoons capers, washed
6 tablespoons green olives, seeded and cracked
2 tablespoons tomato purée
1 bay leaf
1 pound medium to large shrimp, peeled
salt and pepper to taste

Heat olive oil in a 4 quart saucepan and sauté pepper, onion and garlic until soft. Add cho tomatoes, capers and olives. Simmer 15 min Add purée. Simmer 15 minutes more. Add bay and shrimp. Bring to a boil, then lower heat and mer for 20-30 minutes. Add water as needed. S over fresh egg fettucine or spaghetti. Garnish lemon slices. Serves 6.

Recipes by Jay Bon
Toney's Spaghetti

ou will probably have to find someone to take you to Tony Angello's Restaurant if you are ot a New Orleanian, and perhaps even if you are. In a residential area near the yacht harbor at West End, you will find a brick house that looks just about like every other home in the eighborhood, except that it is a bit larger. You will be handed a menu that has one of the ost complete listings of authentic Italian food that I have ever seen, including Fried Calaari, Canneloni, and homemade Spinach Bread.

Italian Cream Cake

ck butter
p shortening
ps sugar
g yolks
ps cake flour
g whites
spoon soda
b buttermilk
spoon vanilla
all can coconut
b pecans, chopped

am butter and shortening. Add sugar. Beat well. in egg yolks, 1 at a time. Sift flour and soda ner. Add flour mixture and buttermilk alternately gar and shortening mixture. Add vanilla, coconut uts. Fold in stiffly beaten egg whites. Bake in 3 pans in a 350 degree oven for 25 minutes.

n cheese icing for Italian Cream Cake:
ht-ounce package of cream cheese
ck butter
b chopped pecans
x confectioners sugar
spoon vanilla

am the cheese and butter. Add sugar and vanil-dd chopped pecans. Spread on layers and sides.

Ossu Bucco

Buy enough veal shanks to serve 4 people.
2 chopped white onions
2 ribs celery, chopped fine
2 cloves garlic, minced
3 medium carrots, chopped
1 cup chopped tomatoes
2 bay leaves
  pinch of shredded lemon rind
  pinch of orange rind
1 teaspoon fresh thyme, chopped
2 cans beef stock
1 cup dry white wine

Osso Bucco means bone with a hole in it. There is marrow in that hole and that contributes to the delicious flavor of this dish. Brown both sides of the veal shanks quickly, starting with the marrow side down, so it will be up during the cooking and the marrow will not fall out. Sauté chopped vegetables with the simmering bones and then add tomatoes and seasoning. Now add the herbs and seasonings, and finally the beef stock and white wine. You can add more stock or water as you need it. Serve with pasta or rice.

Chicken Tetrazzini

¼ pound butter or margarine
1 cup flour
1 quart chicken stock
2 egg yolks
1 small jar chopped pimento
¼ cup sliced mushrooms
  Mozzarella cheese
  salt and pepper
1 four-pound chicken, boiled, boned, cut into strips
1 cup boiled ham, cut into strips
½ pound spaghettini

Put butter in sauce pan and melt, add flour and cook. Stir slowly until well blended, working out the lumps. Make sure the flour cooks long enough not to leave a "floury taste". Add chicken stock, mix well. Add lightly beaten yolks and stir. Add chicken, ham, mushrooms and pimentos, stirring to mix all ingredients. Fold in spaghettini that has been freshly boiled and drained. Place in casserole dish, sprinkle with shredded mozzarella cheese. Bake until cheese is melted and golden.

Louisiana has always been known for its production of fine large pecans. You will notice th
we do not pronounce them "pe-kans" as they do in the north. The word has a softer sound
Louisiana and comes out more like "pu-cahns." No matter how you pronounce the word, the
are wonderful when combined with a lot of brown sugar (also made here) in pralines (pr
nounced "prah-leens," not "pray-lines"). Exceedingly rich pecan pie is excellent, too.

Perfect Pecan Pie

5 egg yolks
1 cup sugar
1 cup white Karo syrup
1 teaspoon vanilla
3 tablespoons margarine
1 cup broken pecan meats
5 egg whites, well beaten
  pinch of salt

Cream margarine and sugar. Blend in lightly beaten egg yolks. Add syrup, vanilla and pecans and stir well. Fold in beaten egg whites. Pour mixture into unbaked pastry shell and bake slowly at 325 degrees for 1 hour until custard-like in consistency. Serve with whipped cream or ice cream if you wish.

Pecan Pralines

2 cups sugar
¾ cup water
½ tablespoon vinegar
4 cups pecan halves

Put to boil sugar, water and vinegar until syrup makes a soft ball when dropped into a cup of cold water. Put in pecans and cook until syrup forms a hard ball in a cup of cold water. Have ready a large platter or pans greased with butter. Drop large spoonfuls of the mixture about 6" apart and let cool. When hard and cold, run knife under each praline and put on a plate.

Brandy Alexander Pie

1 envelope unflavored gelatin
¼ cup creme de cacao
3 eggs, separated
½ cup cold water
⅔ cup sugar
1 nine-inch graham cracker crust
¼ cup cognac
2 cups whipped cream
  chocolate curls for garnish
⅛ teaspoon salt

Sprinkle gelatin over the cold water in a sauc
Add ⅓ cup of the sugar, the salt and egg yolks.
over low temperature until gelatin dissolves and
ture thickens. DO NOT BOIL. Remove from
Stir in liquids and chill until mixture mounds slig
Beat egg whites until stiff. Gradually beat in re
ing sugar and fold this into the thickened ge
mixture. Fold in 1 cup of the whipped cream.
into the crust and chill for several hours. Ga
with remaining whipped cream and chocolate
(made by shaving chocolate).

Marguerites

Beat egg whites from large eggs. Gradually a
tablespoons sugar for each egg white used and
until stiff. Fold in chopped pecans or walnuts to
individual taste and spread thickly on double
crackers. Bake in a 300 degree oven until
brown. These make marvelous treats for childre
also do very nicely with afternoon tea.

Babas au Rhum or Trifle were often the delicious ending for a sumptuous Creole meal. I have often wondered how the Creole ladies kept their trim waistlines, because all the food was rich or sweet, or both. Trifle is a bit of trouble to put together, but well worth the time spent on it. The Babas were so popular that eventually they could be bought in cans in any little country grocery store. The Cajuns liked them, too. And, of course, the Creoles loved their flaming desserts.

Pots De Creme

is is a very Creole dessert, often elegantly served ttle handpainted porcelain cups with handles d pots (pronounced poes). It is a light custard can be made with many different flavorings.

nall package of semi-sweet chocolate bits
p sugar
ps coffee cream
blespoons strong dripped coffee
ell beaten eggs
aspoons Brandy

ce all ingredients except eggs in blender and run chocolate bits are fine. Place in double boiler and mixture to the scalding point. When mixture has d, gradually add it to the beaten eggs, stirring tantly. Pour mixture into custard cups, set them pan of water, cover pan, and bake in a 300 degree for 10-15 minutes. Chill before serving.

Baked Alaska

und cake
g whites
it vanilla ice cream
blespoon sugar
nce Grand Marnier

ce cake on a tray. Surround and cover it with firm ice cream to form a mound. Drizzle liquer it and place in freezer. Whip the egg whites until then slowly whip in the sugar. Cover cake and ream creation with meringue and quickly brown ot oven. It is possible to place the egg shells in dges of meringue, fill with Grand Marnier, and e. Serve immediately as a spectacular flaming rt. This can be made ahead of time and frozen.

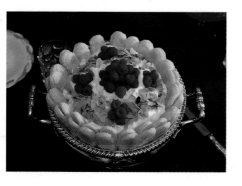

Cherries Jubilee

2 cans dark sweet pitted cherries
1 tablespoon each of sugar and corn starch
¼ cup cognac
1 quart firm vanilla ice cream

Drain cherry liquid into shallow saucepan, or chafing dish Mix corn starch and sugar with a little cherry liquid. Mix with all of the liquid in saucepan. Heat until mixture thickens. Add cherries and reheat. Heat cognac carefully in a small pot. Carefully ignite warm liquid with a match and pour over the cherries while it is flaming. When flame dies down, ladle the cherries over very firm vanilla ice cream.

Trifle

Make a soft-boiled custard with the following:
1 cup (plus) milk
1 cup cream, scalded
3 eggs
¼ cup sugar
⅛ teaspoon salt
1 teaspoon sherry

Beat eggs slightly with a fork. Add sugar and salt. Add milk gradually while stirring. Cook and stir over double boiler but don't boil water. When softly thickened, remove from fire, chill, and add sherry.

To put Trifle together, arrange the following: Place ladyfingers over the bottom of a serving bowl, the more elegant the better. Spread your favorite jam over the ladyfingers. Pour some of the custard over the jam. Sprinkle with sherry and crumble cocoanut macaroons over that layer. Run the whole series of layers again. Top with 2" of whipped cream. Sprinkle coconut on top. Chill for 12 hours.

There are several African-American restaurants in New Orleans that have been around so long that they are almost historic. One of these is Buster Holmes' Restaurant. Pork Chops, Spicy Sausage, and Red Beans and Rice are among the offerings on the menu. These restaurants have always been popular with people of all colors in New Orleans for many, many years.

Mustard Greens

4 bunches of mustard greens (about 4 pounds)
½ pound seasoning ham, diced
½ cup pickled rib tips, chopped
1 cup water
1 onion, diced
½ cup bacon drippings
1 rib of celery, finely chopped
2 pods garlic, finely chopped
4 sprigs parsley, finely chopped
½ teaspoon each of thyme and crushed red pepper
1 teaspoon sugar
   dash of white vinegar

This recipe may also be used to prepare collards, turnips (include cubed turnip bottoms), and string beans.

Clean greens, pull leaves off stems, and soak in fresh water. Put bacon drippings in bottom of pot and heat. Add meat, onions, celery, garlic and parsley. Sauté slowly for 10 minutes. Add cup of water, thyme, sugar, pepper and mustard greens(drained of excess water). Cover pot and cook over medium heat for 1 hour. When tender, add salt and pepper. A dash of white vinegar may also be added. Serves 4-6.

Barbecued Spareribs

2 sides spareribs (cut in sections)
   salt and freshly ground pepper
   salad oil
   barbecue sauce

Place spareribs in large pot. Cover with boiling water. When water returns to boil, reduce heat and simmer for 30 minutes. Remove ribs from pot and place on baking pans. Salt and pepper ribs to taste, then oil ribs lightly and brown both sides under broiler. Place ribs flat in roasting pans and cover with barbecue sauce. Bake at 350 degrees 1-1½ hours or until tender. Baste and turn ribs every 15 minutes.

Sauce:
   1 stick butter
   1 cup onion, finely chopped
   3 pods garlic, finely chopped
   2 cups catsup
   ¼ brown sugar
   1 teaspoon salt
   ½ teaspoon pepper
   1 teaspoon Tabasco
   ¼ cup white vinegar
   1 tablespoon chili powder
      dash of Worcestershire Sauce

Sauté onions and garlic in butter until tender. Add the remaining ingredients and simmer for 10 minutes.

Uncle Sidney's Red Beans

2 pounds dried red beans (fresh)
1 large onion, diced
1 rib celery, diced
8 pods garlic, finely chopped
2 pounds pickled pork rib tips, or smoked shoulder
   of ham, cubed, or smoked ham hocks
1 baked ham bone (sawed in several places)
8 sprigs parsley, chopped
1 bell pepper, finely chopped
3 bay leaves
1 tablespoon thyme
1 stick butter
8 cups freshly cooked hot rice
   salt and pepper to taste

Pick over beans before cleaning (remove bruised or spotted ones). Soak in water overnight covered pot. Add diced onions to beans while are soaking. The following day, strain and pour water. Return beans and onions to pot. Add remaining ingredients to pot, except salt, pepper butter. Fill pot with water, just to cover ingredients. Bring to boil and reduce to a simmer. Season to with salt and pepper. (Not much salt) Simmer for 2½ hours. When tender and creamy, add 1 stick butter and stir in. Serve over boiled rice. (The b improves the texture of the creamy gravy.) S with hot sausage or ham.

Recipes by Chez Hel

Another famous African-American restaurant is Chez Helene's. If you have a healthy appetite and want to eat true "Soul Food," this is your place. The Fried Chicken has a thick batter with spicy seasonings, and the Potato Salad is hot with pepper, too, but delicious. They serve an excellent Creole Gumbo, which is an authentic title because the Africans that worked for the French and Spanish Creoles were also called Creoles. After all, they had come from another country, too. They were called "Creole Gens de Couleur," (Creole people of color) by the French. We forget that the whites who lived on plantations ate soul food, too, but they didn't know to call it that.

Austin's Fried Chicken

cups peanut oil for frying
three to three and one-half pound fryer, cut up
salt and pepper
egg, lightly beaten
cup light cream or half and half
cup water
cup flour

Preheat oil in frying pan to about 350 degrees. h chicken pieces under cold water and pat dry. nkle with salt and pepper. Make egg batter by bining egg, cream, water, salt and pepper. Dip es of chicken first into egg batter to coat and into flour. Add chicken pieces to skillet, meati-parts first. Do not crowd. Turn until browned ll sides. If oil pops, reduce heat. Cook until t is tender and skin is crisp, about 10-12 min-. Serves 4.

Chez Helene's Filé Gumbo

½ pound margarine
1 rib celery
4 sprigs parsley, finely chopped
1 onion, finely chopped
½ cup flour
4 pods garlic, finely chopped
½ green pepper, finely chopped
3 bay leaves
1 gallon shellfish stock or water
½ pound smoked ham, diced
6 crabs (cleaned and quartered)
½ pound hot sausage
½ pound smoked sausage
½ pound shrimp (peel, devein, reserve heads and shells)
1 tablespoon thyme
2 tablespoons powdered filé
  freshly cooked hot rice
  slice hot and smoked sausage into ¼ " pieces

Place margarine in the bottom of a large soup pot, add celery, onion, parsley, green pepper and garlic. Sauté and then simmer for 15-20 minutes over low heat. Add flour and stir constantly for 15 more minutes. Add stock or water and bay leaves. Heat over medium flame for 20 minutes. Stir in ham, crabs, sausages and cook for 30 minutes. Bring to a boil and keep stirring to prevent mixture from sticking. When pot returns to boil, add shrimp, salt and pepper. Allow to return to the boiling point again. Remove from heat and check salt and pepper, adding more if needed. Finally, stir in filé powder. Serve over freshly cooked hot rice. Serves 10-12.

Recipes by Chez Helene's

Kolb's Restaurant is another historic restaurant in New Orleans. It is just across Canal Stree from the Quarter, in the first block of St. Charles Avenue. With its colorful stained glass win dows and an array of German Steins displayed around the walls, the dark wood paneled din ing room gives all of the traditional German appearance one needs to enjoy the very tradition al German menu. Some of the most interesting features are the old ceiling fans, all connecte together by rods and pulleys that date from the first World's Fair that was held in Ne Orleans over a century ago. ♠ Kolb's Restaurant serves traditional German dishes, includin Wiener Schnitzel, Sausage and Wine Kraut, and Apple Strudel.

Sauerbraten Alsace-Lorraine
(Marinated German Pot Roast)

3½ pound, thick cut beef (round is best)
   enough salt and pepper to season properly
      (about 1 teaspoon salt and ½ teaspoon pepper)
8-10 whole cloves
   1 chopped carrot
   2 onions, sliced
   1 rib of celery, chopped fine
1-2 cups vinegar (red wine vinegar preferred)
   1 teaspoon whole peppercorns
2-3 cups water
   garlic and bay leaves

Wash meat and press in the salt and pepper. Place in a Sauerbraten crock or any nonmetal container with the spices and vegetables. Boil water and vinegar together for 2 minutes, then pour over meat all at one time. Cover and place in refrigerator for 2 days.

Drain meat and pat dry. Melt butter (or margarine), 2 tablespoons, in a heavy pot and brown meat on all sides. Pour drippings from the crock over the browned meat. Cover pot. Cook about 3 hours. The easiest way to cook the meat is to put it in the oven at 350 degrees (3 hours). It can be cooked on low on top of the stove, but should be carefully watched and turned.

Now make a gravy with about a cup of crumbled ginger snaps, 2 tablespoons sugar, and 2 cups of the juice from the meat pot. Salt if necessary. Cook until it is as thick as you want it. This is the traditional gravy for Sauerbraten.

This recipe was brought to New Orleans by Phillipe Walther in 1830, and was eventually inherited by Mrs. John Hopper of Louisiana. He eventually settled in "Tigerville," Terrebonne Parish, which later became the town of Gibson. (I added the garlic and bay leaves for Louisiana.)

Austern (Oysters) Kolb

Place 6 oysters on their half shells. Top with lump crabmeat. Salt and pepper. Bake in a 350 degree oven for 7 minutes. Top with Hollandaise Sauce (see recipe on page 12).

Vienna Schnitel
(Wiener Schnitzel - Breaded Veal Cutlet, Viennese St

4 four-ounce white baby veal cutlets
½ gallon frying oil
2 cups buttermilk
2 cups white flour
1 tablespoon black pepper
1 tablespoon cayenne pepper
1 tablespoon salt

Heat oil in heavy pan. Dip cutlets in flour, then bu milk, then bread crumbs. Pound cutlets with the pal your hand when breading them. Fry in hot deep fat golden brown. Serve with lemon wedges. Serves 4.

Eva's Kiss Cake

Place a slice of sponge cake in a bowl, cover wi scoop of ice cream, then another layer of spo cake, and finish with chocolate syrup. This always been a house favorite at Kolb's.

Recipes by K

Shrimp Creole and Shrimp Remoulade (see pictures) are probably two of the most famous Creole dishes in New Orleans, both in homes and in restaurants. You will find the recipes for them in this book. Both are spicy dishes that titillate the palate because they both have a great assortment of different ingredients in them. Each housewife and each restaurant probably has a different recipe for them. The Cajuns do a Tomato, Shrimp, and Corn Soup that is tasty. However, our Oriental residents are also very fond of Shrimp. Trey Yuen fixes Shrimp and Crabmeat in a Cloud, which is quite the loveliest creation I have ever seen.

Trey Yuen Shrimp and Crabmeat in a Cloud

(Trey Yuen on page 52) This is a complicated one, but the result is beautiful. Start with 1 bunch noodles. Heat some oil in a wok and deep fry the noodles until they float up to the top and expand.

ounces medium shrimp (peeled and deveined)
pound crabmeat
cup straw mushrooms
egg whites (well beaten)
cups peanut oil
pound fresh spinach

Marinade:
¼ teaspoon salt
⅓ teaspoon white pepper
1 egg white (well beaten)
1 tablespoon cornstarch
1 teaspoon peanut oil

Seasonings:
¾ teaspoon salt
½ teaspoon sugar
dash of white pepper
1½ teaspoon sesame oil
1 tablespoon cornstarch
(dissolve in 4 tablespoons water)
¼ teaspoon ginger and garlic mix
(coarsely chopped)
½ cup chicken stock
Saki (rice wine) or sherry

Finely grind spinach, extracting juice through cloth napkin. Heat juice. Remove from heat before coming to boil. Skim top. (This green powder is used for coloring shrimp.) Drain powder on coffee filter to absorb excess water. Slice shrimp ¾ of the way along through the outside curve and remove vein. Put in large mixing bowl and sprinkle in 1 teaspoon salt. Mix well, place in colander and spray with cold water. Shake excess water and roll them dry in a kitchen towel. Place shrimp in a bowl. Add spinach extract a little at a time to get desired color. Set shrimp in refrigerator for 20 minutes. Add to shrimp the salt, pepper, egg white and cornstarch, mixing well. Add peanut oil. Mix again. Cover and let marinate in the refrigerator for at least 30 minutes. Heat wok to 275 degrees. Add 3 cups of oil and scatter in the shrimp; stir quickly to separate; toss in straw mushrooms and crabmeat and turn rapidly until shrimp is 80% done. Gently pour 4 well beaten egg whites around wok in a circular motion; swirl 2-3 times until egg white is fluffy. Drain immediately by pouring all contents into a strainer set over a pot. Reheat wok and add 2 tablespoons oil. Toss in garlic and ginger, pressing them in the hot oil. Shower in rice wine. Pour in chicken stock and remainder of seasonings. Pour in dissolved cornstarch and stir vigorously until smooth and glazey. Add the shrimp, crabmeat, and straw mushrooms and give them a few fast folds. Pour into a serving platter. Dress the edges of the platter with crushed rice noodles and serve. *(Author's note: This is the portion that Trey Yuen serves. It will easily serve 2 people. Double the recipe for 4.)*

Trey Yuen presents new ideas blended with the traditional ways of cooking. They buy fresh young alligator meat from an alligator farm, cut it in small white pieces, and cook it with fresh mushrooms and green onions in a typically Chinese light oyster sauce. Trey Yuen means "Crystal Garden."

Oriental restaurants used to be very scarce in New Orleans, but now they can be found in almost every neighborhood. One of the finest was Trey Yuen, which has now moved across Lake Ponchartrain to Mandeville - just a short ride across the Causeway. The Trey Yuen Restaurants are owned by the Wong Brothers, and they produce excellent Chinese dishes, both tasty and beautiful, such as Shrimp and Crabmeat in a Cloud with rice noodles, Steak Kew with Long Beans, and Lemon Chicken, prepared to look like little chickens. The Spring Rolls are made with finely chopped pork and cabbage, and the Barbecued Ribs are perfect. We see the Oriental influence in the state in the Tea House at Live Oak Gardens and the Pagoda at Jungle Gardens.

Lemon Chicken

pieces boneless chicken breast

ce:
      juice of 1 lemon (save peel)
  1 teaspoon arrowroot powder
  1 tablespoon dry sherry
1½ tablespoon sugar
  ¼ tablespoon salt
  1 tablespoon vinegar
  ½ cup water
  2 teaspoons cornstarch
      (mixed with 2 tablespoons water)
  ½ teaspoon peanut oil
  ½ teaspoon minced garlic
      Optional: ½ teaspoon hot pepper oil

inade:
  1 teaspoon sherry
  1 teaspoon light soy sauce
  ¼ teaspoon salt
  1 tablespoon cornstarch
  ½ egg (beaten)

Mix all ingredients for sauce in bowl. Season chicken marinade for 20 minutes. Then dip in flour in another bowl. Heat wok or heavy skillet. Add ½ cup oil. fry chicken until sides are golden brown. Remove skillet. Chop into bite size pieces. Reheat skillet, garlic and simmer for a few seconds, do not scorch. sauce and lemon peel (without white part). When comes to boil, thicken with cornstarch. Remove on peel. Pour sauce over chicken. Makes 1 serving.

Szechuan Spicy Alligator

2 pounds alligator meat (use fresh if you can get it)
¾ cup celery
¾ cup carrots
¾ cup onion
1 cup red or green bell peppers
4 green onions (2" slices)
4 dried hot peppers
⅔ teaspoon garlic (chopped fine)
⅔ teaspoon salt
2 teaspoons sesame seed oil
   crushed Szechuan peppercorns, optional
4 tablespoons sugar
2 tablespoons vinegar, 2 of sherry

Marinade: 3 tablespoons soy sauce
           3 teaspoons cornstarch
           3 tablespoons oil
           ½ teaspoon salt
           ½ teaspoon white pepper
           3 teaspoons egg white

Slice alligator ⅛" inch thick and 2" long, remove fat and gristle. Sprinkle with cornstarch, soy sauce, oil, salt and pepper. Mix thoroughly. Coat with egg white and let marinade ingredients sit for 20 minutes. Cut all vegetables julienne style, about 2-2½" inches long.

Heat wok or heavy skillet until very hot, adding ½ cup oil for 45 seconds over high heat. Drop alligator in hot oil. Stir gently to separate and cook until 70% done. Remove meat from pan and drain oil. Reheat pan with 3 tablespoons of oil. Break dry hot peppers in half into the oil until it turns brown. Add garlic; then add vegetables. Stir-fry for 1-2 minutes. Add alligator back into wok. Add sherry, vinegar, soy sauce, salt, peppercorns, sugar and sesame seed oil. Stir for 30 seconds. Remove from wok to serving platter. Serves 4.

Recipes by Trey Yuen (see pages 51 and 54 for more)

Brocato's is a wonderful ice cream parlor just across St. Ann Street from the lower side of Jackson Square. It is a great place to take a break while strolling about the Quarter on a hot afternoon. The original Brocato's was in another place in the Quarter, and New Orleanians from all over the city drove down there on hot nights for some refreshing Italian Ice Cream. The Brocato grandchildren moved the restaurant to a more central location, but the look is the same, with the white tiled floors and the traditional ice cream tables and chairs. You also have a great view of Jackson Square as you cool off. And over on the corner of the Square, a mule with a hat is trying to stay cool.

Italian Meringue Icing

Have 2 well beaten egg whites ready in a large b Make a syrup by pouring ⅓ cup water, 1 cup sugar, ¼ cup cream of tartar in a sauce pan and boiling it the sugar is dissolved and immediately pour grad in a thin stream into the previously prepared whites. Beat them rapidly and continually until the becomes cool. Get it to a spreading consistency in c to ice the cake. It can be flavored with vanilla, alm frangipane or other liqueurs.

(Brocato's makes marvelous creations out of a st meringue, such as swans and nests to put ice cream in. also have Italian gelatos.)

Beef with Broccoli

1 pound flank steak (cut in 2-3" strips)
2 bunches broccoli (3-4 stalks)
1 teaspoon garlic, minced
2 tablespoons sherry wine

Marinade: 2 tablespoons water
            2 tablespoons soy sauce
            2 tablespoons cornstarch
            2 tablespoons oil
            1 egg white
Gravy Mix: 4 teaspoons oyster sauce
            1 cup chicken broth
            3 teaspoons cornstarch
            2 tablespoons soy sauce
            1 teaspoon sesame seed oil
            2 tablespoons peanut oil
            salt and pepper to taste

   Cut broccoli into individual florets, trim excessive stems. Cut in half if large. Bring 4 cups of water to a rolling boil, add florets and boil for 2 minutes or until crisp. Drain, spray with cold water and set aside. Heat wok over high heat until hot, add 2 tablespoons oil, toss in garlic and beef. Stir in fast, turning and flipping motions until 75% done. Add broccoli and sherry. Stir a few minutes. Stir gravy mix. Pour into the wok. Stir vigorously until thickened. Serves 4.

Recipes by Trey Yuen

Beignets (pronounced (ben-yays) are fried square "doughnuts," (actually more like fritters) made from a dough that is something like French Bread. They have been around New Orleans forever, and are always dusted heavily with powdered sugar before serving. Of course, they must be served with Cafe au Lait (kahfay o lay) - Coffee with Milk. The milk must be boiling and the coffee and milk must be poured into the cup simultaneously, which is an art in itself. You will find them served just across the street from Jackson Square at the beginning of the French Market.

Beignets
(French doughnuts)

op ½ cup of butter and a good pinch of salt into a containing 1 cup of hot water. Bring to a boil and 1 cup of sifted flour. Stir and cook thoroughly it comes together and pulls away from the pan. off heat and add 4 eggs. You must beat after egg you put in. Now the dough is ready to drop deep fat, which should have been raised to 375 ees. As the beignets brown, they will turn over hemselves. Have some heavy brown paper laid and dip them out and onto the paper as they are y. Drain well and immediately sprinkle with dered sugar. They must be served right away, lly with a castor of sugar on the table so that e can be added as your guests turn them over.

Cafe Au Lait

iis is coffee in the French style. Both Cajuns and les like it this way. The coffee is always made from e that is roasted until it is very dark, and often has ory added. The milk is simmered to the boiling t, when tiny bubbles begin to appear around the of the pot. At that point, it is poured into scalding coffee. At the French Market, they pour it out of huge pots, one of coffee in one hand, and one of milk in the other, at the same exact moment. If you very clever and agile, you can learn to do it, too. If you may add the milk to the coffee.

Ratafia of Oranges

The Creole ladies were enamored of their ratafias, particularly to assuage the heat of the humid summers. They were pleasant beverages prepared by the infusion of the juices of fruits, together with flavorings of aromatic substances and a good brandy of French descent.

Grate the zest of 3 oranges, leaving the white pulp behind. Place it in a fruit jar with 2 cups of sugar and a pint of brandy. It is cheaper to make, and just as good, if you use an inexpensive whisky. Set the jar (or several of them) by the kitchen sink and turn it upside down one day, and right side up the next for 1 month. At the end of that time, pour it through a strainer and bottle it for later use. Some people prefer to let it stand for several months before they begin to use it. It just depends on how eager you are. You can make the same thing with peaches, plums or apricots cut in chunks, and removed later to use on ice cream. Leave the kernels in for added flavor. Anise seed, angelica seed or nutmeg can be added for a unique flavor. Experiment with liqueurs. Rum goes well with plums. Mandarin oranges are best.

Anisette

The Creole ladies were also adept at making their own liqueurs. Anisette was fashioned out of a mixture of a dozen drops of Oil of Anise, 3 pints of good alcohol and 4 cups of sugar. A syrup was made of the sugar and 3 cups of water. The anise was dissolved in the alcohol. The two were combined, left to sit a week or two, then strained and bottled.

Down on St. Louis Street and in the rest of the Quarter, everyone knows about Johnny's Po'Boys. He has been catering to the locals for years, and a more pleasant, happy man you will never find. He just loves to create huge sandwiches on French Bread. The name grew out of the Depression years, when a "Po'boy" could buy one of these sandwiches cheaply and make a whole meal of it. One kind, filled with hot crunchy batter-fried oysters with a few dashes of hot sauce, was called the "Peacemaker." Supposedly it was guaranteed to pacify a wife who might be upset because her husband was coming in late. You will be asked by the waiter whether you want it "dressed" or not. Dressed means with lettuce, tomato and mayonnaise. (You will hear people give mayonnaise the French pronunciation in New Orleans - "mi o-nez." Sometimes they don't understand you when you say may-o-naze.)

The Richest Po' Boy

I believe that an overlay of different flavors makes for a richer taste as long as they do not clash. Therefore, I think the combining of ham and roast beef in a large loaf of French Bread is better than just a 1 meat po'boy, and if you add cheese so much the better. It makes an enormous sandwich! It can be be "dressed" the New Orleans way with mayo, lettuce and tomatoes.

The Peacemaker

This name will go down in the history of New Orleans because it was so important for many men. We call it an oyster po'boy or an oyster loaf. It is a po'boy size loaf that is filled with crispy fried oysters. They shouldn't be double battered or they will lose crunchiness. You can also pull some of the bread out of the inside and can put twice as more oysters in. They can be dressed with ketchup, hot sauce, lettuce and tomatoes.

The reason it is called the Peacemaker is because it is absolutely guaranteed to mollify a wife who just may be in a foul mood because she has been waiting up for a late husband. When she smells the aroma of the hot oyster sandwich, she will forget everything she intended to say to him to put him in his proper place, and he can go quietly to bed and get his rest.

Sautéed Crabmeat

The following recipe can be used to serve by itself, in a po'boy, or to serve over a grilled fish.

2½ pounds fresh lump crabmeat
2 cups garlic butter
1 cup green onions, finely chopped

Melt butter in pan over low heat. Add green onions and crabmeat. Stir gently until mixture is hot. Add salt and pepper to taste. Cream sauce can be added.

Recipe by Arnaud's

Po' Boy with Debris

Debris is all of the trimmings and rough bits of that fall off the roast when you slice it. In fact, so good, you can deliberately hack up that roas that you get a lot of debris. When you put it o French loaf with some of the juice or gravy from roast, it is the best thing this side of heaven. first time I heard of it, I was standing in line Mother's Restaurant on Poydras Street with so workmen who were picking up breakfast before go to work. I heard them talking about ordering bisc with "da bri'" and I thought they were talking ab brie cheese. I couldn't quite imagine that they w asking for such a delicate breakfast. I finally watc and figured out they were asking for the debris f the roast to be put on their biscuits with gravy.

n recent years, several old buildings have been turned into four-story malls, and the River-valk has grown out of one part of the World's Fair, so that there are malls all along the Mis-:issippi Riverfront in the downtown area. They are inhabited by shops, restaurants and bak-:ries, and one even displays animals made out of French Bread. The alligator loaf of French 3read is probably the most popular.

Pompano en Croûte

filets of fresh pompano-sliced thin, 2 ounces each
cup scallops, medium
cup finely chopped carrots
cup finely chopped celery
tablespoon chopped shallots
tablespoons heavy cream
eggs - 2 whole, 2 beaten
teaspoon salt
teaspoon white pepper
pinch each of cayenne (red) pepper and nutmeg
cup bread crumbs
sheets frozen puff pastry
cups Peppercorn Sauce (see recipe at right)
parsley sprigs

1op vegetables in food processor until mousse
s. Add carrots, celery and shallots. Blend. Trans-
.o mixing bowl; add cream, eggs, salt, pepper,
nne and nutmeg. Fold gently with rubber spatula.
bread crumbs. Mix thoroughly. Using a fish form
r (8" x 5"), or free hand, cut 12 shells of puff pas-
Center one filet of pompano on each of 6 shells.
:r with ⅙ of the mixture and top with another filet.
h all exposed pastry with the beaten eggs. Cover
second shell. Seal. Form eyes, gills, and scales.
h with more egg. Place on sheet pan. Bake at 375
ees for 20 minutes. When ready, spoon 4 tablens of green Peppercorn Sauce on each dinner
:. Center the shell on the sauce, garnish with
ey sprig. Serve immediately. Serves 6.

Boquet Garni

nch parsley
y leaves
anch fresh thyme
alk celery

e ingredients together with butcher's twine. Use as
ed. (Note: Can be placed in a small cheesecloth bag.)

Green Peppercorn Sauce

2 ounces butter
¼ cup shallots, chopped
1 cup white wine
4 cups fish stock
1 garlic clove, chopped
  Bouquet garni (see at left)
2 tablespoons green peppercorns
  cornstarch
  salt to taste
3 green onions, chopped
1 cup whipping cream

Melt butter in pan over high heat. Add shallots. Cook until transparent. Add white wine, fish stock, garlic, bouquet garni. Reduce to ⅓ volume (approximately 5 minutes). Add green peppercorns and bring to a boil. Reduce heat and simmer for 10 minutes. Thicken with cornstarch until sauce coats spoon. Season to taste. Add green onions. Add whipping cream. Bring to a boil for 5 minutes. Serves 6.

Double Lamb Chops Arnaud

12 domestic, top quality double lamb chops
¼ cup olive oil
1½ cups seasoned bread crumbs
3 bunches watercress
6 cherry tomatoes

Dip chops in olive oil. Coat with herb-seasoned bread crumbs mixed with a little oil. Place chop under broiler. Cook for 7 minutes on each side (for medium). Place 2 chops on each of 6 dinner plates, garnish with a small bunch of watercress and a cherry tomato and serve immediately. Serves 6.

KING CAKES FOR TWELFTH NIGHT

Twelfth Night is celebrated on January 6, which is the twelfth night after Christmas. Since Christmas was a very holy day for the Catholic French, Spanish, and Italians, there was more going to church on that day. Twelfth Night thus became a greater time for celebration. It sig naled the beginning of the Mardi Gras season. In the early days, at the ball that night, the Queen was not previously picked. The King Cake was brought out, a large oval of a sort of coffee cake that was sprinkled with purple, green and yellow sugar, the colors of Mardi Gras Each girl was given a cut piece of the cake, and the piece that had a bean in it designated the Queen. Today, young and old hold parties during Mardi Gras and serve the cake. Whoever gets the bean has to give the next party. Today, instead of a bean, it is usually a tiny plastic baby doll representing the Christ Child.

King Cake

2 envelopes yeast
1 cup coffee cream
¼ cup butter
½ cup sugar
1 teaspoon salt
5 cups flour
2 beaten eggs
  cream cheese or sliced apples

Prepare ¼ cup lukewarm water and dissolve the yeast in it. Add the butter, sugar and half the salt. Cool, but just to lukewarm, and add about 2 cups of the sifted flour. This will make a sort of batter. Now add the yeast and the beaten eggs, using a little of one, and then a little of the other. Beat strongly until the mixture is completely mixed. Now add most of the remainder of the flour with the rest of the salt mixed in it. This should make a dough that is not too stiff. If it begins to stiffen, stop adding the flour.

Lightly flour a board and knead the dough until it begins to look silky. Put the whole mass of dough in a buttered bowl, cover it with plastic wrap and keep it in a warm place. It should rise until it has doubled in size. Remove this dough, which should feel light and roll it into a long sheet, but wide enough to put a

filling in if you wish. The filling is not necessary, in Louisiana, it has become quite popular to mak filling of either cream cheese or sliced apples. If choose to leave it plain or use the apples, dus lightly with cinnamon. Do not use cinnamon v the cream cheese. Roll it up and shape it into a r Coat a cookie sheet with butter and place the rin, dough on it. Make a series of cuts in it at interval:

Bake in a 350 degree oven for 30 minutes or u slightly browned. Ice with a prepared icing and sp kle decorative sugars on it in purple, yellow and g (the colors of Mardi Gras). Don't mix them, but p sprinkle of purple, then yellow next to it, and t green and so on, around the entire ring. Some pe then sprinkle the vary-colored tiny candies on to that. The old-fashioned way was to put a bean in cake, and whoever got it was king for then and to give the next party during the Mardi G season. They now put a tiny plastic baby in it to resent the Baby Jesus, but that could be a hazar someone swallows it. King Cake parties, parades, Mardi Gras Balls continue from Twelfth Night (Ja ary 6) to Mardi Gras (Fat Tuesday), the day be Lent begins, which is a time of fasting.

A table has been prepared by the Cookin' Cajun Cooking School of New Orleans to give us marvelous suggestions for party fare, including French Onion Soup, Pork Chops with Spinach and Pecan Stuffing, Baked Tomatoes with Hot Pepper Jelly and Baked Apples with Raisins, Pecans, and Brown Sugar. All sorts of decorations are displayed for Mardi Gras, and dolls are often dressed as King and Queen.

Mardi Gras Salad

Wash one head of lettuce well, pat dry, and tear into pieces. Slice 1 yellow bell pepper into long narrow strips. Wash ⅛ of a head of purple cabbage. Drain well and slice it thinly into long slivers. Mix a Creole Mustard Salad Dressing by blending with tablespoons of dark Creole Mustard, 2 tablespoons red wine or sherry vinegar, 1 small onion, peeled and quartered, and add salt and pepper to taste in a blender. While blending, slowly pour in oil. Then arrange the salad with lettuce in the bottom of the bowl and purple cabbage and yellow bell pepper strips scattered over the top. Pour ¾ cup dressing over the salad.

Mardi Gras dolls courtesy of Henry Ford of Louisiana

Mardi Gras Pasta

ice red, green and yellow peppers, carrots, and slivers of purple cabbage. Cook a package of ow, green, and white spiral pasta. Stir-fry the etables in olive oil, then add a sprinkling of flour coffee cream with a touch of vinegar and a ll can of V-8 juice to make a light creamy sauce. nkle in some sweet basil, salt, and pepper and ly toss it with the cooked pasta for a colorful for your Mardi Gras table.

Mardi Gras Rice

For a festive dish of rice that is pretty to serve your guests, cut up some red, green, and yellow bell peppers when they are all in season, and some red onions. Sauté them lightly in butter or margarine and stir into freshly cooked rice. Then lightly dust the top of the rice dish with some paprika.

The Old Absinthe House and Pat O'Brien's are both famous spots where a refreshing drink and good company can be found. Some of the most famous creations are Hurricanes, Cyclones, Rainbows, Sazeracs and Frozen Strawberry Daiquiris. The bartenders are well qualified and can mix anything you ask for. A lot of drinks seem to have been named for winds that can blow you away.

Mimosa

Equal parts chilled champagne and orange ju
Serve chilled in a stemmed goblet. Garnish with
orange or lemon slice.

Orange Blossom

1 ounce Gin
1 ounce orange juice
¼ ounce Grenadine

Shake. Serve on the rocks or straight up i
champagne glass.

Strawberry Daiquiri

1 ounce Light Rum
1 ounce Strawberry Schnapps
1 ounce lime juice
1 teaspoon powdered sugar
1 ounce fresh strawberries (frozen ones will do)

Shake with ice and strain into a cocktail gl
Serve with a straw.

Pat O'Brien's Hurricane Punch

4 ounces Dark Rum
4 ounces Pat O'Brien's Hurricane Mix

Serve in a Hurricane Glass (a tall glass) filled with crushed ice. Garnish with an orange slice and a cherry.

Cyclone

2 ounces Vodka
2 ounces Pat O'Brien's Gold Passion Fruit Mix

Serve Vodka and Passion Fruit. Mix in an 18-ounce brandy snifter filled with crushed ice and garnish with an orange slice and a cherry.

Recipes from Pat O'Brien's

Mint Julep

4 sprigs of fresh mint
1 teaspoon powdered sugar
2 teaspoons water
2½ ounces Bourbon

Be sure to use a silver julep cup if you have it. If not, any tall cool drinking glass will do. Muddle the mint leaves with the powdered sugar and water in the bottom of the glass. (You can do this ahead of time and hold in the refrigerator if you are serving a large crowd.) Fill the glass with crushed ice and pour the bourbon over it. Add a mint sprig and put straws in the glass. This drink is for sturdy folk. If you have timid souls, serve them a Mimosa instead.

he new rage in New Orleans drinks is the Magnum that Pat O'Brien's mixes. The enormous lass holds a full magnum of Hurricane, and it arrives complete with enough straws in it for veryone at the table to sip. The historic drinks in New Orleans are the Ramos Gin Fizz and e Sazarac Cocktail.

Ramos Gin Fizz

easpoons superfine sugar
gg white
ash vanilla
lashes orange flower water
easpoons lemon juice
unces half and half cream
unce Gin
easpoons Triple Sec

ake and strain into old-fashioned glass. Henry os concocted this drink in the late 1800's.

Sazarac

unces Rye Whiskey
unce simple syrup

ur into mixing glass with cube ice and add 3 es Angostura and 3 dashes Peychaud bitters. rock glass with Herbsaint. Strain into rock glass dd a lemon twist.

Zombi

ce 151 Rum
ce Grenadine
ce orange juice
ce pineapple juice
ces Collins mix
ash of Apricot Brandy

ve over crushed ice. Garnish with an orange cherry.

Pousse Café

usser" means push, so this is literally a "push ffee" or a coffee chaser, meaning that this drink made from various liqueurs is served after the coffee. The Napoleon House made wonderful ones, but they would not serve it on weekend nights when they were too busy to bother with it.

There is no set recipe because it is all based on specific gravity, and each liqueur has its own specific gravity. If each is poured very carefully down the side of the glass, each will seek its own level, and they make a fantastic drink that is a rainbow of colors. It is lovely served in the evening when you can hold the small liqueur glass up to the light and view the colored layers.

I have found that I can pour each layer more carefully if I pour from a small pitcher rather than from the bottle. If you change brands on one of the liqueurs, it will be apt to have a different specific gravity, so you just have to experiment. The only rule to go by is to put a layer of Grenadine raspberry syrup on the bottom, which is non-alcoholic and cools the mouth at the end of the sipping, and then a layer of clear Cognac on the top.

Here's a list of liqueurs to experiment with. You may want to start out with about 4 layers, and add on as you become more skilled. Have fun!

Triple Sec or Grand Marnier - orange with an orange flavor
Blue Curacao - orange flavor, or blue Creme de Noyaux - almond flavor
Green Creme de Menthe
Pale green Chartreuse
Maraschino Liqueur, white or red - cherry flavor
Brown Creme de Cacao
Goldwasser - clear with gold flecks in it
Apricot Liqueur - orange
Drambuie - light

Where would New Orleans be without the Mississippi? A daytime cruise on the paddlewheel Natchez is a pleasurable, relaxing way to spend a nice part of the day. The food is excellent and music is fine. You will understand more about what a busy place the Mississippi River and how vital it is to the economy of New Orleans. There are other River Boats to ride, and some of them will take you to the zoo at Audubon Park. ♠ A nighttime jazz cruise on the Creole Queen or any of the other boats will put you in a festive mood, and the night air on the Mississippi is filled with cool breezes. The lights come on in the city and across the River Algiers and Gretna, the music is authentic New Orleans Jazz, and the setting is romantic.

Pompano en Papillote

3 medium size pompanos
3 cups water
1 chopped shallot or 2 green onions, chopped
6 tablespoons butter
2¼ cups white wine
1 cup crabmeat
1 cup diced cooked shrimp
1 bay leaf
1½ cups chopped onion
1 pinch thyme
2 cups fish stock
2 tablespoons flour
2 egg yolks
  salt and pepper to taste
½ clove garlic

Clean pompanos and cut into 6 filets, removing head and backbone. Simmer heads and bones in water until there are 2 cups of stock. Sauté filets with shallot in 2 tablespoons butter. Add 2 cups wine. Cover and simmer slowly until filets are t (5-8 minutes). Sauté crabmeat, shrimp and gar 2 tablespoons butter. Add onion and remaining lic. Cook 10 minutes. Add thyme, bay leaf an cup fish stock. Simmer 10 minutes. Melt 2 t spoons butter. Add to crabmeat mixture with stock drained from filets. Simmer, stirring const until thickened. Beat egg yolks and mix with s and remaining ¼ cup wine. Add salt and pe Chill in refrigerator until firm. Cut 6 parchment hearts 12" long and 8" wide. Oil paper well. sauce (divided into 6 portions) on one side of t lay filet on sauce and fold over other half of p Seal edges of paper by folding over and pinc together all around. Lay sealed hearts on an baking sheet and bake at 450 degrees for 15 mi or until paper is browned. Serve at once, cu open paper at table with a sharp knife. Serves 6.

This is one of the most elegant dishes you serve to company. I believe it was first serv Antoine's Restaurant.

Jew Orleanians have so much wonderful fresh fish available to them, that an enormous vari-ty of recipes for fish have been created. Visitors to the city long for the seafood we have, so ou will always find a great variety of fish, shrimp, oyster, and crawfish dishes on every nenu. And chefs all over the city are constantly dreaming up new seafood fantasies, so NJOY!

Pickled Seafood

¼ cup tarragon vinegar
¼ cup lemon juice
½ cup wine
1 tablespoon lemon zest
¼ cup virgin olive oil
¼ cup chopped parsley
1 clove garlic, minced
1 tablespoon rosemary
   dash of Tabasco
   salt and freshly ground pepper

Put all ingredients in an enameled pot and bring to a boil. Let it simmer for 2-3 minutes. Add peeled shrimp, or oysters, or mushrooms, or a mixture, and simmer about 3 or more minutes until they are ten-der. Do not let them get tough. Turn off the heat and let them cool in the mixture. Serve when cool, or hold in the refrigerator.

Grilled Red Snapper

Season red snapper filets or steaks with salt and pepper and tarragon, rosemary, or any other herb you fancy. Coat them copiously with melted butter and put them in a dish so that they can lie in the melted butter while you prepare charcoal fire in the grill. Use a lot of charcoal because you need a lot of heat. Let the grill preheat before you put the fish on, or it will stick to the grill. If your fire is hot enough, you will be able to grill the fish to the proper degree of doneness in about 2½ or 3 minutes on each side. Serve immediately with ½ a lemon for each person.

Trout Filets

-ounce trout filets
p shallots (green onions), chopped finely
p milk
blespoons flour
ht-ounce carton sour cream
ck of butter (margarine doesn't do as well in this)
und lump crabmeat
t and pepper to taste

uté onions in butter until soft. Add flour and th into the butter, but do not brown. Add milk, ng and creaming continuously to prevent lump-Add the sour cream and crabmeat. Remove from Brush filets with butter and place on a greased ng sheet or in a baking dish. Spoon an equal nt of the crabmeat sauce on each filet. Bake 30 tes at 350 degrees. Garnish with parsley, lemon paprika.

And So We Leave New Orleans, as the Paddlewheel Moves Away

As you finish your tour of the city that seems to belong to a foreign country, you are probably too tired, too full of food, and too full of excitement to really relax, but it's all right, because you will carry the memories of it for years to come, and I imagine you will return more than one time.

We will give you one last recipe that is good for all seasons:

Tomato, Shrimp, and Corn Soup

1 tablespoon butter
½ cup chopped green onions
4 ears of corn
2 cans of stewed tomatoes
2 cups small shrimp
1 teaspoon Worcestershire Sauce
¼ teaspoon sweet basil
¼ teaspoon lemon juice
   salt and pepper to taste

Sauté onions in butter until tender. Cut kernels off corn over a large dish with sides. Then scrape cobs, catching all the hearts and milk of the kernels. Chop or process tomatoes. Heat well. Add corn and cook until tender. Add shrimp and other ingredients. Cook until pink and tender but don't overcook. You may want to add a pinch of sugar to blend everything together, but don't make it sweet. Canned shrimp and canned cream corn may be substituted.

Au Revoir,

Bobby Potts

ORDER FORM

If you would like to order additional copies of this book or sample some of our other fine products, please fill out the form below and mail to:

YOUR POINT OF PURCHASE RETAILER
OR
R.A.L. ENTERPRISES
Suite 136, 5000 A West Esplande Ave. · Metaire, LA 70006

TITLE		COST	QUANTITY	TOTAL
COOKIN' NEW ORLEANS STYLE	**64 PGS.**	**$7.95**	_____	_____
New Orleans multi-language book	32 pgs.	$7.95	_____	_____
New Orleans Pictorial Guidebook	64 pgs.	$8.95	_____	_____
Cookin' Country Cajun	64 pgs.	$7.95	_____	_____
Cookin' on the Mississippi (Hard Cover)	64 pgs.	$9.95	_____	_____
Cookin' on the Mississippi (Soft Cover)	64 pgs.	$7.95	_____	_____
Historic Houses of the Deep South	64 pgs.	$12.95	_____	_____
Favorite Recipes from New Orleans	64 pgs.	$7.95	_____	_____
Favorite Drinks of New Orleans	32 pgs.	$4.95	_____	_____
Plantation Country Guide	64 pgs.	$7.95	_____	_____
New Orleans - Crescent City	32 pgs.	$4.95	_____	_____
Best of New Orleans Cooking	64 pgs.	$7.95	_____	_____
Cookin' in High Cotton	64 pgs.	$7.95	_____	_____
Southern Cooking	32 pgs.	$4.95	_____	_____
Recipe Box Cards	Set of 10	$5.95	_____	_____

Postage & Handling ___$2.50___

TOTAL _____

☐ Check Enclosed   ☐ Visa   ☐ MasterCard   ☐ American Express   ☐ Discover

Card Number_____ Expiration Date _____

Name _____

Address_____

City_____ State _____ Zip_____

Daytime Phone (___)_____

All items are satisfaction guaranteed and your purchase will be promtly refunded if returned within 30 days.
Please allow two-four weeks for delivery. No foreign orders please.